# ARNOLD BENNETT: Primitivism and Taste

# ARNOLD BENNETT:
## Primitivism and Taste

By James Hall

University of Washington Press

Seattle: 1959

Selections from the following books are being reprinted by permission of Doubleday and Co. Inc.: *Mr. Prohack, The Card, Helen with the High Hand, The Matador of the Five Towns, Anna of the Five Towns, Leonora, Sacred and Profane Love, The Old Wives' Tale, Clayhanger, Hilda Lessways, These Twain, Riceyman Steps,* and *Lord Raingo.*

823
H14a
37797
July 1959

© *1959 by the University of Washington Press*

*Library of Congress Catalog Card Number: 59-6866*

*Lithographed in the United States of America*

*To Carol*

# Preface

HAVING finished this book, I find other people's remarks on Bennett a little boring. Not untrue, but oblique--to the right or left of center. But there is a history of Bennett criticism. The comments by other novelists have been the most interesting, primarily because one novelist writing about another has an ax to grind. In Bennett's time the ax was technical--point of view and the interior monologue. James saw a great deal of possible life in the Five Towns novels, but discounted it as not rendered--not seen closely through the right kind of observer. Virginia Woolf insisted in an influential essay that Bennett shows all the furniture in Mrs. Brown's house without ever getting inside Mrs. Brown. Forster, like Bennett a less programmatic technician, wrote of the solid achievement and ranked Bennett a little below the best. (One observation of Forster's--that Time is the real central figure of *The Old Wives' Tale*--has become a favorite with later critics.)

For twenty-five years thereafter novelists did not write about Bennett at all. But Edwardian England has become a favorite locale of recent novels, and the age, a symbol of lost powers. The natural impulse has been to reread the Edwardians. Penguin reissued the *Journals* and several novels. And again professional opinion has divided. Angus Wilson finds that, though Bennett's novels theoretically ought to be relevant to current interests, only *Riceyman Steps* interests him. (The choice of the novel about a miser is probably a clue to inter-

preting Wilson's own work. ) V. S. Pritchett ranks *Clayhanger*
and *The Old Wives' Tale* among the important English novels.
John Wain, apparently the only novelist to have read the range
of Bennett's work, attacks the offhand opinion of F. R. Leavis,
"Lawrentian-in-chief, " that Bennett was never disturbed enough
by life to come near greatness: "I think this a pity. How disturbed one has to be before greatness becomes possible, I
don't know, but Bennett has always seemed to me an excellent
novelist, not so inferior to Lawrence as the current fashion
would have us think. "

With one exception, critical books on Bennett date from his
early recognition to a few years after his death--1915 to 1939.
The exception, Walter Allen's *Arnold Bennett* in the English
Novelists series, is the best. About a third of the small book
is biographical, somewhat superseded by Reginald Pound's
sociological biography, and treats Bennett as the novelist
of an emerged, but not yet recognized, industrial middle class.
(This point is essentially undamaged by repetition of Orwell's
belief that, since Bennett came from an industrial region, he
writes about an industrial class. ) But Allen has many less
classifiable insights, especially about the obsession with death
and the creation of a Jungian *anima* in Hilda Clayhanger.

The other book with some interest, though of a specialized
kind, is Georges Lafourcade's *Arnold Bennett: A Study*. His
best points deal with the French sources for the Paris scenes
of *The Old Wives' Tale*.

My own feeling about Bennett now is that "there's no use
raising a shout. " The contemporary attitude in England is indication enough that he ought to be looked at again. Even this
confirmation will be superfluous for that underground group
which has kept him in the Modern Library series during the
years of critical silence. And at least one major university
now gives a seminar in his work.

My indebtedness to previous critics of Bennett is minimal,
but my personal indebtednesses have been cumulative. In the
formulative stage I had a great deal of help from William M.
Sale. I have since talked about Bennett with, and learned about
him from, several friends and colleagues--David Daiches, A.
C. Hamilton, the late Joseph B. Harrison, Robert B. Heilman,
Roger C. Hendricks, Arnold Stein, and Brents Stirling. My

wife, Carol, worked out sections dealing with structure and
symbolism more effectively than I could have done. By the con-
ventional and friendly arrangement, they have all been good
influences and are not responsible for anything the reader may
dislike in the book.


Seattle, Washington                          James Hall
October, 1958

# Contents

# ARNOLD BENNETT: Primitivism and Taste

# 1. Primitivism and Taste

I BECAME interested in Arnold Bennett several years ago while working on an essay on Mann. I read some of the English family novels, expecting to find them about even in quality and dull in general, as were Galsworthy and Wells. But Bennett seemed nearer Mann's starting point and, because he is simpler, more suggestive of later developments in the novel. Still, I did not feel that he had the flexibility and intensity of a first-class novelist and so did nothing with the material. But in coming back to it I decided that he was dramatizing a conflict of significance in the century and, in spite of a manner that until recently seemed old-fashioned, was closer than he has ordinarily been taken to be to a main line of the modern novel.

This conflict develops in the middle-class writer with an admiration for aristocratic values and a counterattraction to primitive ones. The situation which comes more readily to mind is the novelist committed to one set of values or the other. In a scene told in retrospect early in *The American*, Christopher Newman, a speculator, decides suddenly--in a cab on the way to a business deal--that he has made enough money and that his problem has become not to make more money but to do something with what he has. The beginning of the novel shows him in Europe, trying to find and, if possible, buy the answer. The action develops through his discovering how complex an endeavor he has undertaken.

The memorable opposite decision is, of course, Clym Yeobright's to return from Paris with his inchoate plans for Eg-

don Heath--and the action again develops the complexities of
this apparently simple conversion. Class, status, restriction--
the "artificiality and effeminacy" he tried to leave behind in
Paris--count for almost as much on the heath as in the capital. Genealogical tables based on these two decisions--with
James, Eliot, Fitzgerald, Huxley, and Waugh on one side and
Hardy, Dreiser, Anderson, Hemingway, and, say, Steinbeck
on the other--could easily be filled in with the appropriate
names of the last ten years. When, in Trilling's *The Middle of
the Journey*, a woman-in-question says with feeling, "I always
love a fire in a fireplace, " she commits an offense against
manners, morals, and the novel, for people like Laskell and
the Crooms habitually restrain themselves from this sort of remark and place their guest by her failure to do so. The scene
is critical: the error will lead to grosser errors--art-colony
pretensions, badly decorated bowls, elocution, and indelicacy.
Conversely, when Arthur Miller's salesman fails to recognize
that selling is not the equivalent of "primary production, " he
sins against life in a way now less common in the serious novel, but flourishing in the theater, movies, and popular novel.

The recurring conflict between these values is significant.
This book tries to determine its significance for Bennett, but
a suggestion or two in advance may be relevant. Words like
*taste* and *aristocratic* suggest inverted commas and Thorstein
Veblen, but also a meaningful standard. The search for ways
to express the more complex possibilities of the individual is
an effort to establish some higher common denominator of experience. A sense of inadequacy in the daily round produces a
desire to enrich experience and makes taste the ally of expatri-
ation, a striving in a country where the admired values have
more status and tradition for something beyond the homely and
familiar.

Primitivism is a tricky concept and I do not want to define it
for the novel as a whole nor, yet, even for Bennett. But it becomes a dominant line in the novel with Hardy and carries on
with Lawrence and many others. It appears as defense against
defeats and inadequacies felt in civilized living--a way of pro-
testing in the name of the natural against the barriers a civilization sets up against the individual's getting what he wants or
being accepted as he would like to be. Primitivist writers com-

monly express these frustrations through a hero simpler,
"cruder" than the author himself; they try for a lower common denominator of character to symbolize the elemental frustrations. But my interest is less in the naturalism which shows
simple characters living lives shaped by circumstances they
cannot understand or accept, than in the urgency of complex
middle-class characters who want to abandon the artificiali-
ties and restrictiveness of their lives for a simpler, more
natural, usually more forceful way of life. Clym Yeobright
returns to Egdon to escape the artificiality and effeminacy
of the jewelry trade in Paris, Mellors becomes Lady Chat-
terley's gamekeeper, Phillip and Lucy are educated in the
more natural side of Italy in order to return to English society with a new understanding.

Primitivism of this sort and the stylized harmony with nature which we think of as pastoralism are usually considered
opposites, but one characteristic of late nineteenth- and early
twentieth-century novelists is their combination of the two.
Without going into dynamic reasons why this occurs, I am including the two under the one movement.

If these scenes and formulations are as representative as I
believe them to be, we can, for the purpose of looking at Bennett's novels, reduce Tindall's eleven or twelve lines of force
in modern British literature to the lines of force emanating
from the aspiration of the middle class to aristocratic and to
primitive values. A writer like James, or Eliot in poetry,
strives to ally himself with literary and social values which
are beyond debate. Albany and St. Louis cannot easily be lift-
ed to this plane of things-beyond-dispute. The "tradition" must
therefore go beyond one's personal background to larger established values--the British social hierarchy, France, Dante,
a remoter Elyot. Once these have been established, the low
cards can be sloughed. But a writer like Hardy, whose inspi-
ration involves a theory of the universe rather than a set of
manners, interests, and institutions, may find more primitive people useful.

But, after we have drawn up our genealogical tables, some
of the great literature of the times, vitally concerned with the
primitive and aristocratic, remains outside--neither primitive
nor aristocratic, but in various ways attempts to mediate be-

tween the two. Mann, Forster, the early Lawrence, Conrad, and Warren are all, in one way and another, mediators between the aristocratic and the primitive. Into this category, in their lesser fashion, the best novels of Arnold Bennett fall. These men are at home in the two worlds, intensely desirous of reconciling the two by taking the best from both. Ultimately they may not be successful, but they do achieve, albeit sometimes sullenly, working compromises.

If in James and Hardy the extremes are irreconcilable, the history of the mediation shows that a sophisticated primitivism is one product of the aspiration toward taste. The good European is in fact the son of James's American. Little Hanno and Hans Castorp in Mann, Ricky and Lucy in Forster, are a generation or more beyond Christopher Newman. James's middle-class man seeking cultural invulnerability produced in the next spiritual generation--not the same as the next chronological one--the vulnerable middle-class man of Forster, Mann, and Warren. The novelists of the mediation have been the novelists able to move between two levels of middle-class life--encompassing, in a way that neither Trilling nor Arthur Miller does, both the aspiration to aristocracy and the vitality of the primitive.

Definitions of the primitive vary among the mediators as much as among primitivists. But the greatest novelist in the tradition, Mann, has always seen the primitive not in the peasant, the proletarian, or the native, but in the founding bourgeois. This kind of primitivism is a regressive pull, and Bennett, like Mann, sees it as the attitude of a generation which cannot fully enter into middle-class ideals, but looks back toward fathers and grandfathers who apparently held these ideals unthinkingly. The inheritors regard their urban giants-in-the-earth with a mixture of admiration and dissociation. *Buddenbrooks*, *The Magic Mountain*, and *Joseph and his Brothers* reiterate that a natural force dies with the founder of the line and that the problems of the inheritor are equivocal. Mann, of course, develops the conflict so gradually, and so much within the middle-class milieu, that the reader scarcely recognizes it as primitivism at all--hesitates to ally Mynheer Peeperkorn with Quetzlcotl. But, in the "spirit" of the essays and *Joseph*, Mann insists upon a formal method of mediation between the

"dark forces" and the intellect, between primitivism and sophistication. These "dark forces" include far more, of course,
than a relation to fathers and grandfathers, but the regressive
desire is among them. The funeral of Hans Castorp's grandfather, for example, is the first source of the death wish which
culminates in the snow scene. The theological value of the faith
in myth is debatable enough, but the significance of the elaborate attempt at reconciliation is great.

What this mediation between two levels means can be seen
negatively by comparing Mann and Forster with Galsworthy
and Sinclair Lewis, both of whom are highly aware of middle-
class expansionism and both of whom take an unequivocal view.
Galsworthy and Lewis proceed with a minimum of ambivalence.
Lest the reader not comprehend what a Forsyte is, Galsworthy
will define one for him--and does have young Jolyon do so for
Phillip Bosinney. Out of concern for the reader who may not
understand at once what a Babbitt is Lewis demonstrates a
single point through scene after scene. This method may build
up an accurate analysis and report, but it lacks dramatic conflict. Mann and Bennett encompass both the vitality of the
founders and conservators, and the aspirations of their successors to another way of living.

Mann and Bennett have similar starting points and similar
feelings for life. But Mann has been able to use and enjoy the
modes of insight available to the novelist within the past fifty
years, psychological and anthropological, while Bennett,
unwilling to see experience in these ways, stops at a sociological and common-sense view of personality. But Bennett
can be read most profitably, I believe, only in the light of this
tradition of mediation that runs from Mann to Warren. The con-
ventional classification of him as a naturalist confuses what he
believed himself to be doing with what he was actually capable
of carrying out. The birthright of the naturalistic protagonist
is helplessness in the face of overwhelming forces. Clym Yeobright, Madame Bovary, Clyde Griffith, Esther Waters, Nana,
and Studs Lonigan share an extraordinary capacity for being
driven; their ultimate talent is for suffering. But Bennett's heroes and heroines are never helpless. They drive, they are not
driven. However much their actions may be ultimately determined, however little final choice Sophia and Constance may

have, the great thing determined for them is the possession
of a strong middle-class will. The most frequently recurring
scene in the novels is the moment in which Darius or Sophia
or Hilda or even Edwin realizes the miracle of his career--
that he has willed it to be so and it has been so. The triumphant will constantly defeats the naturalistic theory and prac-
tice which Bennett believed himself committed to.

Bennett's aspiration to aristocracy forms an unstable combination with an appreciation of middle-class vitality to produce the odd ambivalence of *The Old Wives' Tale* and the Clayhanger trilogy. The combination is necessarily unusual, and always in danger of disintegrating. In spite of a considerable inflexibility of mind and a passion for penetrating the psychologi-
cally obvious, Bennett at his best is thus one of the mediators
between two great modern worlds. To say so is not to claim
for him a position equal to Mann's or Forster's but to indicate
that his novels should be read in another light than that of naturalistic regionalism.

One significant pattern may suggest this larger context. The
most recurrent and surprising plot in Bennett's novels is the
journey to a "lower land" of freer manners and morals--exile
and return. In a way this is not surprising at all; the return
of the lost brother, son, father, or mother has resolved situations in thousands of potboilers. But something more directly
related to the Joseph myth is, in various disguised forms, one
of the most important elements in *The Old Wives' Tale* as well
as in the Clayhanger trilogy. Mann treats exile and return
openly as myth in Joseph, of course. Bennett, less knowledge-
ably, uses myth with the realistic turn it has normally taken in
the novel.

The myth is pre-eminently suitable as a middle-class one,
just as the Prodigal Son has a pre-eminently upper-class tone.
The prosperity in a foreign land, the rejection of passion in
favor of getting on, and the triumphant return or rediscovery
with wives and cattle, all can be glorifications of middle-class
drive, concentration, and craft. And the very need for success
in the foreign land prescribes a cultural interfusion never offered by success in the homeland. Mann's use of the story is
avowedly a celebration of the bourgeois. The fundamental characteristic of Joseph in Egypt is his determination to stand by

the values of his fathers, and the fundamental fact is his external Egyptianization.

Bennett's best-known use of this myth is Sophia, who ranks somewhere below Joseph, but well above the thrillers. For Sophia, unlike Constance, is, in genesis, a structural character; the conception began, Bennett tells, with Constance and only later encompassed Sophia. Why? Partly, of course, to point up the same two aspects of Five Towns temperament that Annie and Sally represent in "The Death of Simon Fuge." But for that, the flight to France and the long exile would have been as superfluous to *The Old Wives' Tale* as they would have been to "The Death of Simon Fuge." Sophia widens the world of the region--her life and her return are a tribute to the Five Towns and a tremendous commentary upon them. Sophia is, though less self-conscious and largely unperceptive, an agent of mediation between taste and primitivism, between foreign standards and settled regionalism. Sophia in modest fashion represents the "Discovery of Europe"; like Joseph, she retains a contempt of the foreigner and a determination to maintain the essential ways of the fathers, but like Joseph she is so subtly modified by the long residence abroad that she is no longer suited to the earlier way of life. The "buried question of domicile" dramatizes around a simple question the clash of two civilizations.

Sophia is thus a double character, the representative of middle-class vigor and drive, a commercial picaresque heroine; and at the same time a woman with the European experience. The force of her personality is ultimately on the side of middle-class vigor; she does not have the receptivity of the Jamesian character to the European experience, and the comment of taste upon her stage of the cultural advance is made by Dr. Stirling, by the hotel, and by the traveler from Paris. Sophia provides a perspective for Constance, but Dr. Stirling and the hotel milieu provide a perspective for Sophia.

Through Hilda, the Clayhanger trilogy evolves a more complex use of exile and return. This persistence of the Joseph myth in Bennett's work, as in Mann's, is not accidental. (Bennett and Mann emphasize ultimately the hero's rise; James deals most effectively with cultural interpenetration.) The myth of the journey to the lower land to bring the vigorous but mor-

ally and culturally unified hero to the land of sophistication and
complexity is pre-eminently suited to being the myth of middle-class aspiration to taste and power.

The succeeding chapter will develop in Bennett's work these
two interlocking symbolic actions--the regressive desire for
return to a simpler world and the myth of exile-and-return ex-
pressing the universal wish to achieve supremacy over the mature environment. These desires can work at any literary level, of course--Hans Christian Andersen and Horatio Alger as
well as Hardy and James. The serious novelist, having set up
his drama of wishes, must face the contradictions and im-
pediments which acting on them brings out. The critic's problem is to trace the isolated elements of the mediation between the two in the early work, examine the moments of equilibrium in the best novels, and define the disintegration which
occurs when this equilibrum gives way to unsuccessful one-
level symbols of the aristocratic or, obversely, unsuccessful one-level symbols of the primitive.

## 2. Some Bennett Archetypal Patterns

THE MAJORITY of Bennett's novels are far worse than the reader familiar only with his best will readily imagine. Though few of his mystery, wish-fulfillment, and titillating-question-of-the-day novels are worth individual discussion, the patterns and characters of the group are extremely important. Bennett rightly said that he never wrote about anything which did not interest him, and the interests which appear in the inferior work are significant caricatures of those in the serious work.

I

He was uplifted and happy now for the simple reason that he had caught the romance of the doctor's idea of taking idleness seriously and practising it as a profession. If circumstances forced him to be idle, he would be idle in the grand manner. He would do everything the doctor had suggested, and more. . . . In the pursuit of idleness he would become the busiest man in London. . . . Inevitably, unavoidably, he was the new rich. Well, he would be the new rich thoroughly. *[Mr. Prohack]*

As he looked at her, listening and responding intelligently now and then, he saw that Mrs. Capron-Smith was in truth the woman that Ruth had so cleverly imitated ten years before. The imitation had de-

11

ceived him then; he had accepted it for genuine. It
would not have deceived him now--he knew that. Oh
yes! This was *the real article* that could hold its own
anywhere. . . . Switzerland! Switzerland in winter!
He divined that in her opinion Switzerland was not
worth doing--in the way of correctness. But in winter! . . . *[The Card]*

Mr. Prohack's decision and Denry's appraisal suggest different stages of the theme which recurs most frequently in
Bennett's novels--the millionaire's quest. Yvor Winters has
said that James wrote so often of millionaires because in them
alone he found men who, freed from the responsibilities of
earning a living, could direct entire attention to the moral
problem and act with a maximum of moral freedom. The new
man of leisure with money hanging on his hands was a subject
for more than one potential idealization, and James was not
alone in recognizing him. James's conception of the problems
changed with his own experience, becoming more subtle, more
ambiguous. Chad Newsome, with his complex obligation to
Strether and his rarefied taste for art, is not the millionaire
of *The American* who said, "I want the real thing, " and set out
to buy a countess and the best pictures. This earlier millionaire reflects a coarser James occupied with a relatively simple problem. If this earlier American does encounter the morally complex, he encounters it as an outsider. The problems
are not his, nor the solution. When he gives up his countess,
it is not by his own choice. He is acted upon, not acting, in an
intricate dance of European mores and scruples. Only later,
in novels like *The Ambassadors* and *The Golden Bowl*, are
there millionaires whose scruples and moral decisions become the primary consumers of time in the long afternoons on
the expensive hotel terrace (still Bennett's hotel, though not his
millionaire).

The problem which James sets out for Christopher Newman--
and even for Daisy Miller--is what to do with the newly pur-
chased time which they have the rest of their young lives to
spend. Newman and Daisy themselves are very much aware
that this is their problem. In a scene already referred to,
James tells how Newman, the speculator, decides that the

problem has changed, has become not how to make money, but how to occupy the new leisure it makes possible. In Europe he sets out to acquire "the real thing"--a countess and a taste for art and the refinements of civilized living that inherited wealth would have made part of his birthright. His methods are typical of James's early millionaires; he tries to buy them. And here he comes against the real problem of the novel--how to acquire a proper taste, a proper wife, and a proper place in society from an already established order which has its own values and is not at all eager to welcome him. "When Europe's effete back is against the wall not a regiment of millionaires can turn its flank, " one of Bennett's early millionaires discovers.

This problem of the raw, the innocent but vital American, offering a hand still red with the copper dust of speculation to an insolently assured European, occupied the early James as it did not occupy the later. This is not Chad Newsome's problem; we are given to understand that all that has been taken care of before the beginning of the book. But it is Christopher Newman's problem, and very painfully so. In spite of surface appearances, it is Daisy Miller's. And Isabel, in *A Portrait of a Lady,* comes to the continent from unmentionable Albany to buy sorrow and taste in her American-Italian who is even more exclusive than the Europeans, and thus the most successful of them all.

Bennett's best version of the millionaire's quest is the history of Edwin Clayhanger, who is not quite a millionaire and not quite a man of leisure. (Bennett's compromise in his best novels between taste and the founding bourgeois made him give Edwin the aspirations, but not the area of maneuver, of the less respectable millionaires. ) But the clearest demonstration of the pattern occurs in *Helen with the High Hand.* Helen persuades a rich uncle to set out on the road to taste and, as a first step, to absorb the inherited culture which clings to the ruined walls of Wilbraham Hall:

Decidedly it was worthy of the mighty reputations of the extinct Wilbrahams. The Wilbrahams had gradually risen in North Staffordshire for two centuries. About the Sunday of the Battle of Waterloo they were

> at their apogee. Then for a century they had grad-
> ually fallen. The house, grounds, lake, and fur-
> niture (save certain portraits) were now on sale
> . . . it was the symbol of the death of tone and the
> triumph of industrialism.

Installed in Wilbraham Hall, Helen's uncle goes on to Handel, brass bells, and Mrs. Prokter--the proper wife for the new man.

The millionaire's quest is the problem not only of Edwin Clayhanger and James Ollerenshaw; it runs through Bennett's work at every stage--in *The Grand Babylon Hotel, Loot of the Cities, The Card, The Regent, The Lion's Share,* and *The Vanguard.* It is even the problem of Lord Raingo, although the difference between his mind and the minds of James's later characters is a measure of the distance that separates the later Bennett and the later James. But the early James and the early Bennett share a deep commitment to the cultural rise of the middle class. James's Mrs. Medwin and her em-ployer have no more scruples about admitting their object, and no more censure from James, than Helen and her uncle in their struggle toward a room with a view. And James is as sympa-thetic toward Maggie Verver's attempts to buy, not only a prince, but the love and loyalty of that prince, as Bennett is toward Nella, in *The Grand Babylon Hotel,* in her effort to free her prince from a mesh of intrigue and to claim him for her own by right of cash. By the time of *The Golden Bowl,* James was working with a far more subtle millionairess than Nella would ever be. But in 1906 and 1912 Bennett was still more concerned with what Osmond Orgreave could teach Edwin than with what Lord Beaverbrook could tell Lord Raingo.

Lawrence and Forster turn the millionaire's quest in the op-posite direction. Gerald, in *Women in Love,* is a millionaire with problems similar to those of Bennett's and James's mil-lionaires, and he passes through some of the same stages; he acquires the ancient house as the "symbol of tone"; collects clever and intellectual friends of ancient lineage (the Sitwell-ian Hermione); purchases the proper mate (Gerald buys the artistic Gudrun just as Bennett's millionairess in *The Lion's Share* purchases the Parisian musician, Musée); and searches for a vital and articulate life which his money makes possible for him to imagine, but does not help him find. For Gerald, however, taste in art, manners, and morality is not enough. He is looking for something else and, in *Women in Love,* does not find it. He looks for it in Birkin, who has enough subtlety to be a James hero, and in Gudrun, who combines the excitements of the Parisian-taught bohemian with the earthy simplicity inherited from a background similar to the Five Towns; and he dies because he cannot find this something else. He is looking for a primitive ultimate which the protagonists of later novels like *The Plumed Serpent* believe themselves to have found.

Forster's Lucy, in *A Room with a View,* is also a millionairess in the sense of being comfortably free from the scramble for money; like the others, she goes abroad for the "European experience"; and, unlike James but very like Lawrence, she learns that the representatives of taste, Cecil and the clergyman, have taken the wrong direction, that the right direction is the Simple Life lived with the modified and suburbanized primitive, George Emerson.

Bennett, too, came to feel that taste was not enough and in his later novels redefined the aristocratic in terms that have commanded few literary followers. But the millionaire's quest constitutes one of the most important elements in the structure and meaning of *The Old Wives' Tale* and the Clayhanger trilogy.

## II

One of the nineteenth century's most durable legacies has been the relevance of architecture and the architect as symbols of taste. A fair history of the modern novel could be done in terms of these two symbols, beginning with the great houses thrown up in the early twentieth-century novel (in *Buddenbrooks, A Man of Property, Tono Bungay,* to begin near the turn of the century), including the architects who are good characters (a desirable lover for Irene Forsyte, a receptive philosophic vessel like the naval architect Hans Castorp, the quaint but desirable father like Gumbril Senior), and picking up such metaphorical use of architecture as Lawrence's in *The Rainbow.*

The whole history could be brought down to the present in terms of the "stately homes of England" novelists like Evelyn Waugh and Elizabeth Bowen (the hero of *Brideshead Revisited* is, significantly, a painter of stately homes, since the rules forbid including any house built after 1800 in the stately homes class); and the cultural lag in America could be symbolized by seeing the Crooms's Connecticut cottage as the good house, and the architect, again significantly, as a writer on low-cost housing and slum clearance.

The novels are usually quite explicit on the reasons for the houses, but the multiplication of architects--unless they result simply from the demand for houses--is a somewhat more subtle matter. Why is the architect so desirable to some novelists as lover, thinker, establisher-of-a-suitable-background? Because the architect is the perfect mediator between middle-class origins and vitality and the aspiration to aristocratic manners and standards. In him the trinity of middle-class aspiration is made flesh; he is an artist, but by necessity an artist with more of the engineer than the bohemian about him; he is a businessman (Gumbril Senior complains sadly about the constant necessity for negotiating but Mr. Orgreave is a sharper dealer than Darius Clayhanger); and, because of the special prestige of architecture in the hierarchy of taste, he is a member of the social elite and possibly a key to it. The emergence of the architect as protagonist and father-image follows from a literary law of supply and demand. A "tremendous pent-up demand" existed for this mediator between taste and commerce, and the good architect was created to meet the demand. (The physician has an analogous role as the most practical and prestigious scientific man.)

Bennett's architects are strategically placed at the three significant stages of his writing. Brindley, in "The Death of Simon Fuge, " "The Matador of the Five Towns, " and other early stories, represents, along with Dr. Stirling, the best taste in the Five Towns--a taste with some strength in literature, music and "the Wedgwood, " but prone to confusing girders and paintings. In the best novels, the architect-as-father-image (Mr. Orgreave) and the practical scientist (Dr. Stirling) are fundamental to a management of perspectives which Bennett was never again able to achieve. When Bennett's

last architect, young George Cannon, the son of Hilda Lessways, goes off to war, his departure leaves wartime London
to the commercial picaresque hero; the hotel manager and the
big-time financier take over the world which only the architect
had restrained them from taking earlier.

The practical scientist, Dr. Stirling, appears first in the
stories as the Brindleys' friend and reappears for a crucial
role in *The Old Wives' Tale*. The physician is, of course, almost the perfect analogue: he is the businessman-as-man-of-
science, as the architect is businessman-as-artist, and like
the architect he has entrance to the established classes. And,
as Brindley and Orgreave add music to their professional qualifications, Dr. Stirling has added literature--with even a special taste for French novels. Functioning at first to round out
the picture of Five Towns taste, he later serves as one of the
main devices in *The Old Wives' Tale*.

For Bennett, the female of the practical artistic class is the
actress, occasionally the writer. He tried the actress again
and again, but without producing a remarkable success. The
actress has certain obvious qualifications: she is an artist of
sorts, is in touch with the world of writers and dramatic production; she has a possible access to the upper classes through
sex, though she is more likely to draw the *nouveau riche*; but
her roots in the business tradition are weak, and Bennett was
never able fully to utilize her as a symbol of mediation. She became increasingly frequent, in fact, in the period of his decline. (Bennett's woman novelist, Carlotta, has shallow roots
in the Five Towns, but mostly lives in a world of art-colony ecstasy.)

### III

To complete the Bennett pattern, we need to add to the Quest-
er and the Mediator a representative of the vigor which made
the quest possible. Darius Clayhanger, Sophia, Lord Raingo,
and Hilda and even Samuel Povey are all manifestations of the
character whom, in his extreme form, Bennett called the Card.
The incarnations of this commercial picaresque hero--in both
male and female form--are worth looking at.

Even in Bennett's best novels there is a strong strain of what

might be called the commercial picaresque. Some of his most
lovingly treated men and women parallel the rise of a Tom
Jones or a Moll Flanders or a Roxana, with this difference--
Bennett's characters do not rise through a series of adventures
in the lanes and parks of England, but in an atmosphere of the
black market and the ticker tape. The successful speculator
is the hero of many Bennett novels; his quaint ways, his "cardishness, " are recounted with loving relish. Denry becomes
the Old Adam, and leaves spiritual sons to inherit the top spot
in many a late Bennett book; but the unsuccessful speculator is
a villain and, like John in *Leonora,* must expect to die while
his wife and chattels pass on to better businessmen.

*The Card* is the best of Bennett's commercial picaresques.
Starting his career as a man of business by cheating in school
(and who doesn't? Bennett inquires mildly), Denry goes on to
forgery of a mild order, usury, exploitation of a shipwreck,
and ingenious social climbing. At no time is he under the least
restraint from Bennett, who shares with Fielding and Defoe a
lack of prudery and moral concern for the decisions of his
characters.

*The Regent* (American title: *The Old Adam*) takes Denry
through further exploits which include the stabilizing of a tot-
tering playhouse and the fabulous search, in the wilds of America, for just the right actress to play the leading role in his
play. Everything Denry touches pays, and this is enough for
the early Bennett. That he never saw great reason to change his
mind is shown by his later feeling for *The Card* as one of his
four best books. (*The Card* might almost, if the plot were not
so thick, be included among such manuals as *How to Live on
Twenty-four Hours a Day,* for it explicitly recounts just the
proper phrases for getting on in every circumstance.)

What distinguishes this commercial picaresque from the titan
of an author like Dreiser, is the relish with which Bennett out-
lines the road to success. He depicts no passion-ridden figure
stalking toward doom, but an old-fashioned rogue whose nights
are innocent of remorse and whose days are cheerfully amoral.

His early children's serial, *Sidney Yorke's Friend,* strikes
the note which recurs through Bennett's later books, by no
means excluding *The Old Wives' Tale* and *Clayhanger.* It
is a pure success story, and was followed by other stories

of the successful financier or manager. There is the inscruta-
ble hero of *Hugo,* whose success is outshone only by that of his
counterpart, the Evelyn of *Imperial Palace* (while Hugo contents himself with managing only one department store, Evelyn
manages a merger of hotels). We learn that, if he chose, Hugo
could be a successful statesman rather than the manager of a
department store. *Teresa of Watling Street* presents an extremely sympathetic portrait of a financier, and Mr. Prohack,
though he is somewhat more troubled by money than the average
Bennett hero, has affinities to Denry the Audacious, and to
Bennett himself, in his attempts to make the best use possible
of the golden time money has bought for him.

In *A Great Man,* Bennett carries the commercial picaresque
into literature. And in such novels as *Lilian, The Price of
Love,* and *Helen with the High Hand,* he shows that the Bennett
heroine is as adept as the young businessman in getting on,
though her charm may suggest an easier way. The indomitable
ladies of Bennett's lesser novels, more akin to Moll Flanders
and Roxana than to Clarissa Harlowe and Pamela, are distin-
guishable even in the "fine, careworn face" of Sophia and the
proud face of Hilda Lessways, so that even if they were not interesting in their own right they would be as sisters of Bennett's greatest women.

Helen, heroine of *Helen with the High Hand,* differs from the
other commercial protagonists in some methods, but not in her
goals. She is never in danger of losing her virtue, since she
chooses to exploit an old man, her own uncle, but engages in
every feminine counterpart to Denry's exploits. Starting with
the 1911 equivalent of a pickup on a park bench, she hires herself out as her uncle's housekeeper after getting the real housekeeper fired; rifles his cashbox and extracts an additional hundred pounds when he protests about the theft; forces him to
leave his life-long home for a Buddenbrookish great house
which fits into her plans for social advancement; and finally,
marries the man of her choice after breaking up his match with
the sister of her best friend.

Throughout this story, Bennett treats Helen with courtesy and
affection. She is just a high-spirited girl, in essence not very
different from the more impressive Sophia, herself a black-
marketeer.

A James heroine like Fleda Vetch can be depended upon in a crisis to choose the road to victory that is moral rather than commercial, but Bennett's heroines gain no such awkward insights. In *The Price of Love,* Rachel, a servant-companion to a wealthy old invalid, like Fleda, aspires to marry into the family. No unfortunate scruples stop her, and she does marry Mrs. Maldon's nephew, Louis. With him she shares a life which, though annoyingly complicated by his chicanery, is at least smoothed by Mrs. Maldon's money.

*Lilian* is Bennett's *Moll Flanders.* With Moll she shares both a tendency to be easily seduced, and the ability to land on her feet. Discharged as a typist, she is for a time kept by the brother of her former employer. When she becomes pregnant, her lover marries her (on the Riviera), dies of pneumonia, and leaves her a large fortune. Her triumphant return to her home town consists in taking over the office where she had been an employee, and thus confounding her sister-in-law. The rewards of vice are sweet. In the commonplace but delicate lineaments of Lilian are traces of Denry the Audacious. Even Carlotta of *Sacred and Profane Love* is in some respects a picaresque heroine, but the first-person narration obscures this identity with sentimental and moral scruples and insights.

Bennett's actresses and women of talent shade over easily into courtesans; for a man who was not preoccupied fundamentally with the problems of sex he has a surprising number of stories about them. *The Pretty Lady,* however, is not a commercial picaresque; preoccupied with the civilian's side of a major war, Bennett here does not recount a courtesan's rise to power, but uses her as a vehicle for exposés of governmental graft and as the center of some researches into religious phenomena. Reneé, the French light woman of *Whom God Hath Joined,* is not a triumphant picaresque heroine, but a rather human sinner treated with a good deal of sympathy; and Delphine, the mistress of Lord Raingo, gets nothing for her sins but remorse that culminates in suicide. Nevertheless, these women are sports in the Bennett cosmology; the typical Bennett heroine is Lilian, on the potboiler level; Helen, in the intermediate novels; and Hilda or Sophia, on the level of the serious novels--a highhanded, proud, and forceful woman who uses life far more often than life uses her.

Where does this leave Constance of *The Old Wives' Tale*,
and Anna of the Five Towns, and Leonora? They are not like
the strong-minded women but they are equally important to the
structure of Bennett's books. The fact is that, except for their
sex, they are not very different from Samuel Povey and Bennett's other male conservative amassers of wealth. Bennett accords his quiet amassers of wealth a measure of respect, but
he never gives them quite the love and sympathy that he gives
to his cards and speculators. At best, they receive the tactful
and slightly supercilious handling accorded to Samuel Povey.
At the worst, they are as ruthlessly handled as the miser of
*Riceyman Steps*.

Even more unfortunate in losing Bennett's regard are the unsuccessful speculators. To speculate, to succeed, to spend,
those are the *sine qua non* of the Bennett world; but there is
also the uncle we don't talk about, the nephew who had to flee to
America, the father, husband, or brother who had to kill himself. The smile at Lilian's triumphant return to her home town
becomes only a shake of the head and a disapproving frown for
Titus Price, who embezzles money in *Anna of the Five Towns*;
for the unsuccessful George Cannon of *Hilda Lessways*; for
John, the unfortunate husband in *Leonora*, who has to commit
suicide to make way for the successful second husband.

But even when unscrupulous speculators are found out, if they
are quick-witted or strong enough to save themselves, Bennett
has few harsh words for them. In *The Statue* (written with Eden
Phillpotts), Bennett's Crampiron escapes retribution because
his money is needed to stir up a European war necessary to
England's interests; in *Teresa of Watling Street*, Craig, who
has been coining silver for years and is an acknowledged felon,
is permitted to escape by detectives who have found him out,
because he has had the quick-wittedness to be the father of two
beautiful daughters. There is no necessary censure for the
caught speculator, providing he plays his cards right. But the
Bennett eye is upon him, and he must make good or suffer.

The speculator, the card, is thus the dominant commercial
character in Bennett's novels. Conservative middle-class characters like Constance are relevant to the side of Bennett that
has long been recognized, but the particular significance of the
millionaire's quest, the card, and the architect lies in their

use alongside the recognized elements to give, in Bennett's best work, that sense of competing views of life so evenly balanced that they are in almost perfect equilibrium. Bennett never understood the forces in this equilibrium, and was able to maintain it for only a very short period. After the Clayhanger trilogy the card's victory over the conservator and the architect becomes more and more complete, until by the time of *Lord Raingo* and *Imperial Palace* not only does no Constance fumblingly find her seat at a Parisian restaurant, but no Dr. Stirling inquires of the state of French literature and no visitor at the Savoy is so rude as to ask about the Comédie Française, or the English chaplain.

## 3. Taste and the Region

IT IS easy to catalogue regional novels which, whatever their superficial differences, share a single-mindedness rare in other kinds of literature. *Babbitt* uses the region for satire, *The Grapes of Wrath* for sympathy with kindly folk abused by the economic order, *God's Little Acre* for the exhibition of interesting new mammals discoverable in a march through Georgia. Each hammers at a single quality. The author's attitude is fixed and unambiguous; character, dialogue, structure, and the rest are chosen to produce slight variations on a foreordained effect.

Bennett's mediation between the primitive and the aristocratic, the range of his sympathy from the strength of the working middle class and the second-generation aspiration to more rarefied manners and tastes, demands a more equivocal attitude. "The Death of Simon Fuge, " an early novelette, spells out in obvious characters and obvious dialogue, the fundamental positions in this attitude. The views of life at work in "The Death of Simon Fuge" are check points for the views that compete in *Anna of the Five Towns*, *The Old Wives' Tale*, and *Clayhanger*. The story is long enough to permit these perspectives to be worked out in detail, and its very crudenesses make the perspectives overt.

Bennett's best novels have three levels: the level of the man who has undergone "the European experience"; the level of the commercial, nonconformist middle class; and an intermediate level of the more cultivated or experienced Five Townsman--

Brindley in the early stories, Sophia, Edwin, Hilda, and the
Orgreaves. In "The Death of Simon Fuge" these levels are laid
out diagrammatically; in the later novels they are compounded
into a structure more complex than critics have realized. The
position of the cultivated outsider, so often presented by impli-
cation or by intrusions of the author in later novels, here has
its representative in the narrator, Loring--born in Devonshire,
educated at Cambridge, and, as an official of the British Museum, culturally guaranteed. The intermediate level has three
representatives--Brindley, Dr. Stirling, and Colclough. All
represent the aspiration to taste: Brindley and Colclough with
their interest in music, Brindley in his chairmanship of the
local museum committee and his books, Dr. Stirling with the
largest collection of books in the Five Towns. Colclough, with
his expensive new automobile from Paris, represents, moreover, the mechanical progress of the new generation. Both
Five Towns families of this intermediate level (Dr. Stirling
is an outsider, an Edinburgh man) are still close to the founding bourgeois generation, as Brindley makes clear to Loring:

> You told me once you knew Exeter. Well, this isn't
> a cathedral town. . . . Both my grandfathers were
> working potters. Colclough's father was a joiner
> who finished up as a builder. If Colclough makes
> money and chooses to go to Paris and get the best
> motor-car he can, why in Hades shouldn't his wife
> ride in it? If he is fond of music and can play like the
> devil, that isn't his sister-in-law's fault, is it? His
> wife was a dressmaker, at least she was a dress-
> maker's assistant. If she suits him, what's the mat-
> ter?

The "dressmaker's assistant," Mrs. Colclough, and her sister
Annie, the "superior barmaid," represent the third level--the
uncultivated, though respected, woman of the Five Towns.
    Bennett's elementary strategy, like James's, is to bring to-
gether the representatives of these different civilizations. *

---

*In the important novels, Bennett's most frequent device is a

Loring the cultivated outsider, comes to Bursley as the guest
of Brindley, an architect. A newspaper obituary of Simon Fuge,
the *avant-garde* painter who had been born in the Five Towns,
turns Loring's visit into a Jamesian detective mission to dis-
cover the reality behind Fuge's famous parlor story:

> There was a special reference in the Gazette obit-
> uary to one of Fuge's most dramatic recitals--a nar-
> ration of a night spent in a boat on Ilam Lake with
> two beautiful girls, sisters, natives of the Five
> Towns, where Fuge was born. Said the obituarist:
> ''Those two wonderful creatures who played so large
> a part in Simon Fuge's life. ''
>         This death was a shock to me. It took away my en-
> nui for the rest of the journey. I too had known Simon
> Fuge. That is to say, I had met him once, at a soi-
> rée, and on that single occasion, as luck had it, he
> had favoured the company with the very narration to
> which the Gazette contributor referred. I remem-
> bered well the burning brilliance of his blue-black
> eyes, his touching assurance that all of us were nec-
> essarily interested in his adventures, and the ex-
> tremely graphic and convincing way in which he
> reconstituted for us the nocturnal scene on Ilam Lake
> --the two sisters, the boat, the rustle of trees, the
> lights on shore, and his own difficulty in managing
> the oars, one of which he lost for half-an-hour and
> found again. It was by such details as that about the
> oar that, with a hint of humour, he added realism
> to the romantic quality of his tales. He seemed to

_____

version of exile-and-return--the long sojourns of Sophia in
Paris and Hilda Lessways in Brighton, Anna's shorter but
similarly significant trip to the Isle of Man, Arthur Twenlow's
return after many years in New York. The resemblance to
Mann's use of the myth is not merely superficial: Mann and
Bennett are dealing, on however different levels, with the
same process--the effect of a complex and established civilization.

have no reticences concerning himself. Decidedly
he allowed things to be understood. . .! Yes, his
was a romantic figure of one to whom every day,
and every hour of the day, was coloured by the vio-
lence of his passion for existence. His pictures had
often an unearthly beauty, but for him they were
nothing but faithful renderings of what he saw.
My mind dwelt on those two beautiful sisters. . . .

Once Loring has determined to possess the reality behind this
possibly scandalous idyll, he faces the double problem of eval-
uating the Five Townsman as witness, and of collecting the relevant testimony. His discoveries about Brindley, his guide,
are equivocal. Brindley, who on a visit to the British Museum
had been "dressed like a self-respecting tourist" and had
seemed "quite deferential and rather timid, " at the Knype station appeared "anxious to be mistaken for a sporting squire.
He wore very baggy knickerbockers, and leggins, and a cap.
This was apparently the agreed uniform of the easy classes
in the Five Towns; for in the crowd I had noticed several
such consciously superior figures. " On the platform Brindley's
decisiveness jolts Loring out of his "mood of gentle, wise condescension. " Brindley, Loring discovers, is neither the primitive nor the London variety of museum official, but the cultivated man of the Five Towns, an aggressive Edwin Clayhanger. The clothes, the aggressiveness, the positiveness about
the niceties of freshly rolled cigarettes, the unwillingness to
bow before metropolitan opinion about the superiority of the
*Gazette* to the *Manchester Guardian,* and the surprising knowl-
edgeableness about music, books, and painting force Loring
to revise his estimate of the Five Towns as "shabby, undignified, rude. "
    This first treatment of the region is of a sort to please those
writers who used to call on the novelist to recognize its "culture" as well as its commercial and farming vigor. The man
from London has been surprised, the reader's sympathy has
gone over to the vigorous representative of Five Towns culture, and Simon Fuge is under suspicion of having been a complete liar. But, before the investigation proper begins, Bennett inserts the most skillful structural element in the story--

a visit to "the Wedgwood" which tests Brindley and Dr. Stirling, the representatives of Five Towns taste, against the museum's one Simon Fuge:

> The thing was not much more than a sketch; it was
> a happy accident, perhaps, in some day's work of
> Simon Fuge's. But it was genius. . . . It killed ev-
> erything else. But wherever it had found itself, noth-
> ing could have killed it. . . . And it glowed sombrely
> there on the wall, a few splashes of colour on a mor-
> sel of canvas, and it was Simon Fuge's unconscious,
> proud challenge to the Five Towns. And not merely
> was it his challenge, it was his scorn, his aristo-
> cratic disdain, his positive assurance that in the bat-
> tle between them he had annihilated the Five Towns.

Against this standard, Dr. Stirling and Bob Brindley lose stature; Dr. Stirling, whose collection of books is even larger than
Brindley's, has sold his two Simon Fuges; and Brindley shows
more interest in the Wedgwood's girders and scholarship cups
than in the Simon Fuge--which, he says, was given to the gal-
lery by a man who had won it in a raffle:

> "Now you see this girder, " Brindley said, looking
> upwards.
> "That's surely something of Fuge's, isn't it?" I
> asked, indicating a small picture in a corner, after
> he had finished his explanation of the functions of
> the girder. . . .
> "Which?" said Mr. Brindley.
> "That one. "
> "Yes, I fancy it is, " he negligently agreed. "Yes,
> it is. "

In a crude but effective way, Bennett restores Simon Fuge
to his London position, makes him once more the painter known
to coteries all over the world, and places Bursley's finest taste
by its indifference to the modern. The investigation sets Simon
Fuge, at the height of his reputation, against the representatives of Bursley's third--uncultivated--level.

Loring's investigation completely debunks Simon Fuge the
parlor roué. One of the sisters has the Bennett "instinct for experience" and has wide experience in the world--as a barmaid
at a private bar: "I had not expected . . . to see an odalisque,
an houri, an ideal toy or the remains of an ideal toy; I had not
expected any kind of obvious brilliancy, nor a subtle charm
that would haunt my memory for evermore. On the other hand,
I had not expected the banal, the perfectly commonplace."
But Annie Brett does not completely rule out the possibility that
Simon Fuge has told a version of the truth; for when she hears
that he is dead:

> There were tears in her reddened eyes. . . . Those
> moist eyes caused me a thrill. There was after all
> some humanity in Miss Annie Brett. Yes, she had
> after all floated on the bosom of the lake with Simon
> Fuge. The least romantic of persons, she had yet
> felt romance. If she had touched Simon Fuge, Simon
> Fuge had touched her. She had memories. Once she
> had lived. I pictured her younger. I sought in her
> face the soft remains of youthfulness. I invented
> languishing poses for her in the boat. My imagina-
> tion was equal to the task of seeing her as Simon
> Fuge saw her. I did so see her. I recalled Simon
> Fuge's excited description of the long night in the
> boat, and I could reconstitute the night from end to
> end. And there the identical creature stood before
> me, the creature who had set fire to Simon Fuge,
> one of the "wonderful creatures" of the *Gazette*,
> ageing, hardened, banal, but momentarily restored
> to the empire of romance by those unshed, glittering
> tears.

But the next moment Annie moves off to argue with a commercial traveler about the new legislation on barmaids, and her
practiced insincerity makes Loring agree with Brindley's ver-
dict that her tears are "purely mechanical."
But if Annie can be conceived "even now, speciously picturesque, in a boat at midnight on a moonstruck water," Sally Colclough, the wife of the pottery manufacturer with the expensive

French automobile, is the Constance of the pair--a solid, fat,
family woman whose house shows "far more money and consid-
erably less taste" than the Brindleys' and who could never have
been even speciously picturesque.

> In Mrs. Colclough there was no coquetterie, no trace
> of that more-than-half-suspicious challenge to a man
> that one feels always in the type to which her sister
> belonged. The notorious battle of the sexes was as-
> suredly carried on by her in a spirit of frank mus-
> cular gaiety. . . . Put her in a boat on the bosom
> of the lake under starlight, and she would not by
> a gesture, a tone, a glance, convey mysterious
> nothings to you, a male. She would not be subtly
> changed by the sensuous influences of the situation;
> she would always be the same plumb and earthly
> piece of candour. Even if she were in love with you,
> she would not convey mysterious nothings in such
> circumstances. If she were in love with you she
> would most clearly convey unmysterious and solid
> somethings.

Annie's testimony is equivocal, but Mrs. Colclough's is unquestionably accurate--and devastating. She not only lacks the at-
tractiveness and tone necessary, but she has thorough realistic
memories:

> "I asked him if he could row, and he was quite
> angry. So we went, to quiet him. . . . I was just
> thinking how he got his feet wet in pushing the boat
> off. . . . Someone came down to the shore and
> shouted to Mr. Fuge to bring the boat back. . . .
> I shall never forget how funny he looked in the moon-
> light when he dropped the oar. . . . I assure you
> he kept on talking about neckties. I assure you, Mr.
> Loring, I went to sleep--at least I dozed--and when
> I woke up he was still talking about neckties. But
> then his feet began to get cold. I suppose it was be-
> cause they were wet. The way he grumbled about
> his feet being cold! . . .

'It was the annual outing of the teachers of St.
Luke's Sunday School and their friends, you see.
. . . Well, I don't know what you call all night. But
I was back in Bursley before eleven o'clock, I'm
sure. "

The only thing Loring is able to get out of Mrs. Colclough is a
"certain self-consciousness" at the suggestion that Annie knew
Simon Fuge well, but the Brindleys dispose of this suggestion
with laughter at breakfast the next day.

The matter-of-fact atmosphere of the Five Towns completely
negates the "possibility of ineffable indiscretions on the part
of Simon Fuge" which had interested Loring. The vigorous hon-
esty of the region has cut the *avant-garde* artist down to size.
But the ambivalent returns in the unexpectedly pat ending:

"A strange place!" I reflected, as I ate my dinner
in the dining-car, with the pressure of Mr. Brindley's steely clasp still affecting my right hand, and
the rich, honest cordiality of his au revoir on my
heart. "A place that is passing strange!"
And I thought further: He may have been a boast-
er, and a chatterer, and a man who suffered from
cold feet at the wrong moments! And the Five Towns
may have got the better of him, now. But that portrait of the little girl in the Wedgwood Institution is
waiting there right in the middle of the Five Towns.
And one day the Five Towns will have to "give it
best. " They can say what they like! . . . What eyes
the fellow had, when he was in the right company!

In James's stories of artists and writers the conflict is most
frequently between the real and the meretricious in art. Bennett's clash is between art and the bourgeois conception of life
--between the reality of the imagination and the reality of the
unimaginative. The struggle is between the cultivated--the talent of Simon Fuge--and the primitive--in the Mannian, bourgeois sense of the primitive. The resolution gives each side
victory in its own terms; the critic has the Simon Fuge in the
Wedgwood and Bursley has its facts about the night on Ilam

Lake. Simple and highly patterned as all this is, it nevertheless expresses the double standard which gives Bennett's best work its range and makes him a genuine, if never a perfect, mediator between primitivism and taste.

# 4. Manners, Morals, and the Five Towns Predicament

BENNETT'S three most important novels before *The Old Wives' Tale--Anna of the Five Towns, Leonora,* and *Sacred and Profane Love*--constitute an informal trilogy which graphs the significant points of his cultural curve. Bennett recognized this relationship, calling Anna the "uncultivated woman, " Leonora the "cultivated woman, " and Carlotta the "woman of genius" of the Five Towns. All three novels deal with the Five Towns predicament and its solution-- *Anna of the Five Towns* most thoroughly with the predicament, *Leonora* with predicament and solution, and *Sacred and Profane Love* with solution.

## I

*Leonora* is a wish-fulfillment novel, and *Sacred and Profane Love* is so undeviating a celebration of the artistic life that Bennett added a "tragic" ending, Carlotta's death by appendicitis at the moment of her greatest triumph, to make the book acceptable to the public. But Bennett's second novel, *Anna of the Five Towns,* conforms to the conventions of the naturalistic novel. The ostensible plot of the book (the miser father making Anna an accomplice in driving to suicide Titus Price and that financial Tess, Willie Price) is almost wholly conventional-- Zolaesque, Goncourtesque, Hardyesque. Anna and Henry Mynors watching Willie trudge home between the abandoned pit-shafts is a scene straight out of Wessex, and the President of the Immortals hovers not far above the concluding sentences:

Her thoughts often dwelt lovingly on Willie Price, whom she deemed to be pursuing in Australia an honourable and successful career, quickened at the outset by her hundred pounds. This vision of him was her stay. But neither she nor anyone in the Five Towns or elsewhere ever heard of Willie Price again. And well might none hear! The abandoned pitshaft does not deliver up its secret. And so--the Bank of England is the richer by a hundred pounds unclaimed, and the world the poorer by a simple and meek soul stung to revolt only in its last hour.

Anna, barely a consciousness, is the low point from which a steady rise in self-awareness, an increasing play of mind, continues through *Hilda Lessways*. Here Bennett is as far as he ever was from getting Virginia Woolf's Mrs. Brown. The proportion of furnishing--interiors of the Tellwright home, interiors of the Sutton home, views of Bursley, views of the pottery works, views from the Isle of Man --is higher than in any other Bennett novel of comparable worth. There are correspondingly fewer real scenes than in the best work; neither the quality of life evoked through small crises nor the preparation for larger crises compares with Bennett's later skill in handling these structural blocks.

The meaning and vitality of the novel do not lie, therefore, in any gratuitous expansion of Anna's consciousness, but in her predicament and her choice between the two ways of life which are being urged upon her. Anna is a *tabula* not quite *rasa*; something is written but much space is yet to be filled; she is creator of the role which Edwin Clayhanger plays with so much more self-awareness and distinction: the young person to be fought for by a parent and a parent-substitute who represent two levels of the cultural curve. Anna is the first Bennett character to face the Five Towns predicament: the restrictiveness and, even more, the rudeness of life which the founder, the Ephraim Tellwright or the Darius Clayhanger, stands for, set against the "instinct for experience, " as Hilda Lessways calls it--but here, as in *Clayhanger,* really the instinct for better manners, better tastes, less commercialism, a fuller even more than a freer life.

Ephraim Tellwright, the symbol of the rude and the restric-
tive, is a character whom Bennett never in the early novels
draws without respect, without even awe and a curious inverted sympathy. Ephraim's strength is his single-minded force
of will. His original sin is not the active evil which his hard-
ness in money matters causes but the sin which Bennett treats
in "The British Home" in *Paris Nights*--lack of style, igno-
rance of the most elementary manners, purposeless restraint
of all joy.

> This surly and terrorising ferocity of Tellwright's
> was as instinctive as the growl and spring of a beast
> of prey. He never considered his attitude towards
> the women in his household as an unusual phenome-
> non which needed justification, or as being in the
> least abnormal. . . . If you had talked to him of the
> domestic graces of life, your words would have con-
> veyed to him no meaning. If you had indicted him for
> simple unprovoked rudeness, he would have grinned,
> well knowing that, as the King can do no wrong, so a
> man cannot be rude in his own house. If you had told
> him that he inflicted purposeless misery not only on
> others but on himself, he would have grinned again,
> vaguely aware that he had not tried to be happy, and
> rather despising happiness as a sort of childish gew-
> gaw. He had, in fact, never been happy at home: he
> had never known that expansion of the spirit which is
> called joy; he existed continually under a grievance.
> The atmosphere of Manor Terrace afflicted him, too,
> with a melancholy gloom--him, who had created it.
> . . .
> The next morning his preposterous displeasure
> lay like a curse on the house. . . .

Anna's involvement in her father's moods--her *modus vivendi*
with his angers, her ability to detect the first signs of their
lifting, her impotent early stratagems for dealing with them--
combines with Tellwright's own gruff humor to make him a
meaningful, and sometimes even likable, figure in a way that
Earlforward, the miser of the late novels, never is. But

the rude, single-minded life of Ephraim, the founder of a line, symbolizes the grim smile of the Five Towns; and Anna, the heiress, is ready for her own version of the millionaire's quest.

What Anna finds is the Suttons. And the Suttons, for all their "large photogravure of Sant's 'The Soul's Awakening,'" in the dining room, are for Anna symbols of a remarkable degree of cultivation. When, under the sponsorship of Henry Mynors, she accepts the invitation to the sewing meeting, she discovers for the first time a cultural level entirely different from the milieu of Ephraim Tellwright. She discovers a world where the use of money rather than the puritanism of money rules. Beatrice Sutton paints and has had voice training; Alderman Sutton is genial and bantering to young ladies; Mrs. Sutton is motherly and understanding and tactful. The furniture is better than anything Anna has yet seen:

> The splendour of Mrs. Sutton's drawing room was a little dazzling to most of the guests. . . . That fact was that the luxury of the abode was mainly due to Alderman Sutton's inability to refuse anything to his daughter, whose tastes lay in the direction of rich draperies, large or quaint chairs, occasional tables, dwarf screens, hand-painted mirrors, and an opulence of bric-a-brac. The hand of Beatrice might be perceived everywhere, even in the position of the piano, whose back, adorned by carelessly-flung silks and photographs, was turned away from the wall. The pictures on the walls had been acquired gradually by Mr. Sutton at auction sales; it was commonly held that he had an excellent taste in pictures, and that his daughter's aptitude for the arts came from him.

In this society Anna feels the inadequacy of her own manners and conversations:

> [Mynors] talked gaily with Beatrice and Mrs. Banks: that group was a centre of animation. Anna envied their ease of manner, their smooth and sparkling

flow of conversation. She had the sensation of feeling vulgar, clumsy, tongue-tied; Mynors and Beatrice possessed something which she would never
possess. . . . Anna lost confidence in herself; she
felt humbled, out-of-place, and shamed.

Before Anna leaves the Sutton's house for the first time, she
and Mrs. Sutton have entered into the mother and daughter relationship which eventually defeats even formidable Ephraim
Tellwright and which determines the structure of the novel.

The first part of the novel thus sets up the relationship between Anna and her father; "The Sewing Meeting" sets up the
relationship between Anna and the mother-substitute; much of
the remainder of the novel is the struggle between these two
parents over Anna.

Mrs. Sutton invites Anna to go on the vacation to the Isle of
Man, and somehow persuades old Ephraim to permit the trip.
This creates the need for new clothes that leads to Anna's first
outright defiance: the cashing of her extra dividend check. "He
was enraged; but since his anger was too logical to be rendered
effectively coherent in words, he had the wit to keep silence."

This vacation trip is Anna's equivalent to Sophia's trip to
Paris with Gerald Scales, Hilda's trip to Brighton with George
Cannon: "It overwhelmed her, thrilled her to the heart, this
revelation of the loveliness of the world." She sees not only
Liverpool and the Isle of Man, but a new level of manners and
sympathy.

During breakfast--a meal abundant in fresh herrings,
fresh eggs and fresh rolls, eaten with the window
wide open--Anna was puzzled by the singular amenity
of her friends to one another and to her. They were
as polite as though they had been strangers; they
chatted amiably, were full of goodwill, and as anxious to give happiness as to enjoy it. She thought
at first, so unusual was it to her as a feature of domestic privacy, that this demeanour was affected,
or at any rate a somewhat exaggerated punctilio due
to her presence; but she soon came to see that she
was mistaken.

After the return from the Isle of Man, she is Mrs. Sutton's daughter, not Ephraim's daughter nor Henry Mynors' fiancée. In the crisis over whether to deliver Willie Price into her father's hands for forgery, she cannot argue with the old man or ask for the help of Mynors. "There was only one person from whom she could have asked advice and help, and that wise and consoling heart was far away in the Isle of Man." Her final break with her father--the final resolve to live no longer in her special version of the Five Towns predicament--involves an issue which Mrs. Sutton has already been consulted on:

> "What's afoot now?" he questioned savagely.
> "I must buy things for the wedding--clothes and things, father."
> "Ay! clothes! clothes! What clothes dost want? A few pounds will cover them."
> "There'll be all the linen for the house."
> "Linen for--It's none thy place to buy that."
> "Yes, father, it is."
> "I say it isna', " he shouted.
> 'But I've asked Mrs. Sutton, and she says it is."

Against this unanswerable logic of Anna's spirit, Ephraim is defeated and turns over forever her checkbook and passbook. The great victory has been won, and Willie Price's misfortune, beside this, is merely a misfortune, a defeat for an unsuccessful speculator. The condemnation of Anna to a marriage in which she will not only be able to mother Henry Mynors, but will be on still more intimate terms than before with the Suttons is one of those victories which Bennett's more vigorous heroines habitually achieve.

As the novel develops Anna recognizes a second side to her predicament: the original static life under the domination of Ephraim shades into a future made up of the forceful financial life which goads Titus and Willie Price to suicide. Her second-generation sense of morals as well as of manners rebels. As the Suttons bring to a climax her rebellion against Ephraim's manners, the Prices bring to a climax her rebellion against his morals. Once these two families have been introduced for what they are, the structure of the novel consists in their parallel claims upon Anna's interest leading to the parallel defiance by which she establishes her independence.

Anna's moral objection and its crystallization around the Prices is the aspect of the novel least like Bennett--a residue from an earlier naturalism. The later Bennett characters who face the Five Towns predicament object on the ground of manners; for them, manners are morals. But once Anna--simpler mind who finds her symbol of taste in an old Wesleyan woman--has gone to the works in Edward Street and seen the dirty, outmoded factory and the harassed owners, Ephraim for her is tainted with the misery of Titus and Willie Price. Anna's pity for Willie--the only love she is capable of--is her attempt to make peace with the ghosts of her father's evil. Bennett never presents Willie with the skill necessary to make him seem worthy of Anna's emotion, but, by a remarkable twist, he does turn Titus Price, who, as the Sunday School Superintendent, has been nothing more than a broad satire on Wesleyanism, into something more by contrasting his clownish conduct of the Sunday School picnic with the ignominy of his suicide:

> The town was profoundly moved by the spectacle of this abject yet heroic surrender of all those pretenses by means of which society contrives to tolerate itself. Here was a man whom no one respected, but everyone pretended to respect--who knew that he was respected by none, but pretended that he was respected by all; whose whole career was made up of dissimulations: religious, moral, and social. If any man could have been trusted to continue the decent sham to the end, and so preserve the general self-esteem, surely it was this man. But no! Suddenly abandoning all imposture, he transgresses openly, brazenly; and, snatching a bit of hemp cries:"Behold me; this is real human nature. This is the truth; the rest was lies. I lied; you lied. I confess it, and you shall confess it. "

The problems raised by Anna's aspirations are carried on in *Leonora* and *Sacred and Profane Love*. The superiority of

*Anna of the Five Towns* is, in part, the superiority of naturalistic conventions to wish-fulfillment ones; but its great superiority lies in its firmer presentation of the alternatives and
its suggestion, achieved by heavy and occasionally even wood-
en methods, that Anna's predicament is the predicament of the
Five Towns--and, beyond the Five Towns, of a stage in an industrial, commercial, middle-class civilization. Anna is the
simplest level at which Bennett handled the problem of the aspiration to the aristocratic.

By the standards of "the European experience" Anna's aspirations are not high. The Suttons, Wesleyans though they
are, are recurring symbols of our second level, the cultured
families of the region. (At the end of *These Twain*, in fact, Edwin explicitly allies the Suttons with his other culturally respectable Bleakridgeans--the Orgreaves, the Brindleys, Tom
Swetnam, and Dr. Stirling.) But to Anna the Suttons mark an
immeasurable improvement in manners and taste over Ephraim
Tellwright. A symbolism of light and darkness, done in un-
abashed naturalistic descriptions, identifies Ephraim, the
lender who has no more direct connection with manufacture
than Alderman Sutton, with the smoke, filth, and oppression
of the potteries and Mrs. Sutton with the light, airy, sail-
boating atmosphere of the Isle of Man. Anna knows more what
she is going away from than what she is going toward, but
with her creation Bennett himself moved a step toward developing the conflict which he was best able to handle.

II

*Leonora* begins with the rudeness and restrictiveness of
Five Towns life even in suburban Hillport, and ends, significantly, with the solution of exile. The novel is almost a fable
of middle-class aspiration, but it develops in its heroine a
more complex and cultivated sensibility than Anna's.

Leonora's external problem is to substitute for an undesir-
able husband (an unsuccessful speculator, in terms of our ar-
chetypes) a desirable one (not quite an architect, but an Amer-
icanized importer of fine pottery and a man of taste and refined
sensibilities). John Stanway, the unsuccessful speculator, is
ostensibly a pottery manufacturer, and Leonora's position

fluctuates between respectability derived from her husband's
position and humiliation at the community's increasing knowledge of Stanway's losses in "stocks and shares. " Stanway's
operations appear to Leonora the equivalent of habitual drunkenness; he is as engrossed in his failures as Ephraim Tellwright in his successes. He is, as a husband, frequently in-
considerate, and regularly uncommunicative. Leonora views
him with detachment, sees herself as a woman who has thrown
away her life on a man not financially and spiritually worthy
of her, and, in the first half of the novel, reflects continually
on this fixed pattern of her life. She is resigned to the spiritual
unworthiness, but no Bennett heroine can tolerate an insolvent
husband. When Stanway's finances reach the point where he
wants first to mortgage and then to sell her house, she refuses
and drives him to a convenient suicide. (In the same way,
Sophia's final break with Gerald comes when he demands that
she write her family for money. )

The beneficiary of this suicide, Arthur Twenlow, is another
businessman-as-man-of-taste-and-refinement. However, he
has done his commercial building in another sphere--New
York--and appears in the novel as a man of leisure, revisiting
the town from which he had run away many years earlier. Presumably he transacts bits of business during his absences from
Hillport, but the reader sees him as the millionaire looking for
the finer things and finding them in Leonora. His respectable
and unassailable wealth, his leisure, his interest in Leonora's
daughters, and his respect for the more refined emotions make
John Stanway's harassed gruffness and undignified wheedlings
infinitely reprehensible to Bennett's Nora. Stanway's suicide
ends Leonora's imprisonment in herself and leads to life in
London with Prince Twenlow.

At the outset Leonora is a sort of low-grade Virginia Woolf
heroine caught in a well-furnished novel. Her problem is the
problem of the woman of forty restrained by all the conventions of her world. Reality to her means the living out to its
end of a fixed pattern of life--the husband all too comprehensible without being really comprehensible at all, the young lovers
passing before her in the streets and on the lawn. But she has
the Bennett "instinct for experience":

She knew her world and its men and women. She was
not too soon shocked, not too severe in her verdicts,
not the victim of too many illusions. And yet, though
everything about her witnessed to a serene temperament and the continual appeasing of mild desires . . . even now, on her fortieth birthday, she
still believed in the possibility of a conscious state
of positive and continuous happiness, and regretted
that she should have missed it.

The absence of this "positive and continued happiness" comes
to Leonora most clearly in the contrast with her daughters'
vitality:

For a brief moment, vainly coveting the ineffable
charm of Ethel's immaturity, she had a sharp perception of the obscure mutual antipathy which separates one generation from the next. As the cob
rattled into Hillport, that aristocratic and pluto-
cratic suburb of the town, that haunt of exclusive-
ness, that retreat of high life and good tone, she
thought how commonplace, vulgar, and petty was
the opulent existence within those tree-shaded villas,
and that she was doomed to droop and die there,
while her girls, still unfledged, might, if they had
the sense to use their wings, fly away. . . . Yet
at the same time it gratified her to reflect that she
and hers were in the picture, and conformed to the
standards; she enjoyed the admiration which the
sight of herself and Ethel and the expensive cob and
cart and accoutrements must arouse in the punctili-
ous and stupid breast of Hillport.

Leonora's disciplinary crises dissolve into a slightly trans-
parent envelope:

"You've forgotten all that sort of thing, mother."
Ethel burst into gushing tears at last. "Father can
kill me if he likes! I don't care!" . . .

> She was not at all hurt by Ethel's impassioned
> taunt but rather amused, indulgently amused, that
> the girl should have so misread her. She felt more
> maternal, protective, and tender towards Ethel than
> she had ever felt since the first year of Ethel's ex-
> istence. She seemed perfectly to comprehend, and
> she nobly excused, the sudden outbreak of violence
> and disrespect on the part of her languid, soft-eyed
> daughter. . . . The interview which had just termi-
> nated, futile, conflicting, desultory, muddled, ten-
> tative, and abrupt as life itself appeared to her in
> the light of positive achievement.

But Leonora is not a Hillport Mrs. Ramsey. She sees nuances, but does not find in them the meaning of life. Life is
not to go on and on until John Stanway awakes with a cry. The
entrance of Arthur Twenlow and the suicide of Stanway relieve
Leonora of her version of the Five Towns predicament, and
open to her the "luxurious, voluptuous, and decadent civilization" of London. There are still enough higher stages on the
cultural curve to occupy the Five Towns aspirant to the aristocratic. What vitality the novel has disappears with the dis-
solution of Leonora's fixed pattern of life, and neither stock
regional characters like Meshach and Aunt Hannah nor the em-
barrassing scenes of Leonora in love do anything to revive it.
    Leonora needs a fairy prince to rescue her from her Five
Towns predicament. But in the expansion of her consciousness,
her area of self-awareness, Bennett focuses far more clearly
than in *Anna* the fact that the Five Towns are not primarily a
region, but a climate of manners.

### III

*Sacred and Profane Love* proposes the exile of the artist as
a solution of the Five Towns predicament. Carlotta, who begins
as one of Bennett's millionairesses, great-granddaughter of
"the famous potter--second in renown only to Wedgwood, "
from the first never fits into the huge house built by her great-
grandfather, furnished by her grandfather, and "placidly accepted" by her parents--a house where the great walnut piano

"too, spoke of Evangelicalism, the Christian Year, and a dignified reserved confidence in Christ's blood. It, too, defied the assault of time and the invasion of ideas. It, too, protested against Chopin and romance, and demanded Thalberg's variations on 'Home, Sweet Home.'"

The novel wastes only thirty pages on Carlotta's predicament. Thereafter she leaps into a one-night affair with the great pianist Diaz, goes to London and becomes involved with her publisher, abandons this affair to rescue Diaz (now fallen into drunkenness and drug-addiction), and reaches her apotheosis in the performance of *her* opera and Diaz's recovery. The "tragic" ending consumes one page.

Carlotta's "solution" is far more a waving of a wand than Leonora's. The land of Carlotta's exile is not France, as with Sophia, or Brighton, as with Hilda Lessways, but a land vaguely conceived of as the Country of Genius. Carlotta's journey is not a *becoming*, but a translation. One moment she is the girl reading Spencer and Darwin in Bursley, and the next the besought of publishers, the savior of a fallen Rubinstein, and the triumphant conceiver of operas. The waters of the Red Sea of art part and admit a remade Carlotta to the promised land.

*Sacred and Profane Love* eliminates all those planes on which the novel of manners depends. Its most ambitious effort, on which the novel goes to pieces before it really begins, is to tie Carlotta's love for Diaz to Chopin's Fantasia, as Proust ties Swann's to the theme from Vinteuil:

> In the Fantasia there speaks the voice of a spirit which has attained all that humanity may attain: of wisdom, of power, of pride and glory. . . . The voice of this spirit says that it has lost every illusion about life, and that life seems only the more beautiful. It says that activity is but another form of contemplation, pain but another form of pleasure, power but another form of weakness, hate but another form of love, and it is well these things should be so. It says there is no end, only a means; and that the highest joy is to suffer, and the supreme wisdom is to exist. If you will but live, it cries, that grave but yet passionate voice--if you will but live! Were

there a heaven, and you reached it, you could do no
more than live.

It is not that Bennett cannot use music--for comedy or man-
ners--but he cannot wrap Carlotta in the civilizing flag of Chopin and move her from one level of life to another without
leaving any trace of the first level. One has only to set beside
the bathos of the preceding passage the section of *These Twain*
where a group of Bursley suburbanites is trying to take advantage of the civilizing influence of music to see how far from
Bennett's bent *Sacred and Profane Love* is:

> At the close of the last item, two of Brahms'
> Hungarian Dances for pianoforte duet (played with
> truly electrifying *brio* by little wizening Tom Or-
> greave and his wife), both Tertius Ingpen and Tom
> fussed self-consciously about the piano, triumphant,
> not knowing quite what to do next, and each looking
> rather like a man who has told a good story, and
> in the midst of the applause tries to make out by an
> affectation of carelessness that the story is nothing
> at all.
>
> "Of course, " said Tom Orgreave carelessly, and
> glancing at the ground as he usually did when speak-
> ing, "Fine as those dances are on the piano, I should
> prefer to hear them with the fiddle. "
>
> "Why ?" demanded Ingpen challengingly.
>
> "Because they were written for the fiddle, " said
> Tom Orgreave with finality.
>
> "Written for the fiddle ? Not a bit of it!"
>
> With superiority outwardly unruffled, Tom said:
>
> "Pardon me. Brahms wrote them for Joachim.
> I've heard him play them. "
>
> "So have I, " said Tertius Ingpen, lightly but scorn-
> fully. "But they were written originally for piano-
> forte duet, as you played them tonight. Brahms
> arranged them afterwards for Joachim. "
>
> Tom Orgreave shook under the blow, for in musi-
> cal knowledge his supremacy had never been chal-
> lenged in Bleakridge.

"Surely--!" he began weakly.

"My dear fellow, it is so, " said Ingpen impatient-
ly. . . .

Then the eldest Swetnam (who had come by invitation at the last moment) said:

"I'm sure Ingpen is right. "

He was not sure, but from the demeanour of the
two men he could guess, and he thought he might as
well share the glory of Ingpen's triumph.

With all allowances for style and for Bennett's insistence on
the obvious, this corresponds to the use of art and manners
in the early James. In *The American*, Christopher Newman
is liable to the same weaknesses in painting as the Bleak-
ridgeans in music:

Mademoiselle Noémie remained silent; at last
she dropped into a seat. "Well then, for those five
it's fixed, " she presently said. "Five copies as
brilliant and beautiful as I can make them. We've
one more to choose. Shouldn't you like one of those
great Rubenses--the Marriage of Marie de Medicis?
Just look at it and see how handsome it is. "

"Oh yes; I should like that, " he allowed. "Finish
off with that. "

"Finish off with that--good!" she laughed. She sat
a moment looking at him, then suddenly rose and
stood before him with her arms expressively folded."
"Ah *ça*, I don't understand you, " she bravely broke
out. "I don't understand how a man can be so ignorant. "

"Oh, I'm ignorant certainly. " And he put his hands
in his pockets.

"It's too ridiculous! I don't know how to paint *pour
deux sous.* "

"You don't know how?"

"I paint like a cat; I can't draw a straight line.
I never sold a picture until you bought that thing the
other day. " And as she offered this surprising in-
formation she continued to smile.

Newman met it with a grimace of his own. "Why
do you make that statement?"
"Because it irritates me to see a clever man so
*bête*. My copies are grotesque."
"And the one I possess--?"
"That one's the flower of the dreadful family."

The significance of *Sacred and Profane Love* is its failure to
resolve the Five Towns predicament by alchemical transmu-
tation. The important Bennett novels deal with Five Townsmen
attempting to rise one level on the cultural curve and enmeshed
in the immeasurable complexities of that modest ascent. *Anna
of the Five Towns* shows a repressed girl aspiring to the manners and cultivation of the Wesleyan Suttons, but Anna lives
in a world that is made real and in which the choices before
her are firmly embodied in the characters of the novel. *Leonora* shows the predicament of the woman with more mind, with
greater capacity for the spiritually gratuitous, but Leonora
moves in an inadequately realized milieu which fails to give
her problem depth. *Sacred and Profane Love,* a complete failure, bypasses all complexities for a faked solution. But in
these three novels, Bennett enunciates his theme of middle-
class primitivism set against a modest aspiration to more
aristocratic values.

# 5. *The Old Wives' Tale*

BENNETT'S best-known novel, *The Old Wives' Tale*, is a tribute to the strength of the Old Order--to a certainty and vigor deriving from unquestioned codes. This treatment of the Old Order is by no means the Lawrence kind of primitivism. But it is not really paradoxical that primitivism and taste often exist thus side by side, that critics who like James also like Faulkner, or that Bennett is a writer who acknowledges claims of both primitivism and taste. Even *Clayhanger*, his saga of the quest for a larger climate of manners, is made ambivalent by the strikingly sympathetic Darius; and *The Old Wives' Tale* is even more ambivalent, since Sophia's position is often doubtful. But though the victory of primitivism is, in *The Old Wives' Tale*, a partial and a temporal one, it is significant; and in so far as the book has a heroine, that heroine is not Time, but Constance Baines.

*The Old Wives' Tale* presents a softened version of the Five Towns predicament, in which the dramatis personae have significantly changed places. As defenders of the primitive position, instead of grasping Tellwright or driving Darius, there are well-bred Mrs. Baines, "a Syme of Axe, " and her daughter and disciple Constance, frequently referred to by Bennett as "the mild Constance." And as attackers in the name of taste and progress there are not the gentle Anna or the old-maidish Edwin Clayhanger, but Sophia, "that incalculable, untamable, impossible creature, " and Samuel Povey, who looks like "one of those calm quiet ones, " but is really a man of "black, un-

47

governable rages, " as his mild Constance discovers the moment she tries to change him.

The reason for this shift in the Five Towns Players' cast
is that *The Old Wives' Tale* is the story not of a miser and
his daughter, nor of a man like Darius Clayhanger, who "had
risen out of the mass, but . . . was fiercely exceptional";
rather *The Old Wives' Tale* is the story of two mild women
of the commercial class who claim, with some justice, many
qualities associated with the aristocratic--pride of caste, *no-
blesse oblige,* and graciousness. Bennett sees their struggle
to maintain the Old Order across the lapse of one and two generations. By his own Parisian standards the culture of the
nineteenth-century midland town is so low as to put the Baines's
claim in a humorously ironic light. But he likes Baineses,
and he does not deny their qualities.

So *The Old Wives' Tale* has a much gentler tone than the
average Bennett novel, though like his others it is organized
around battles between two opposing ideologies. Unlike Hilda
and Darius and Ephraim, Constance and Mrs. Baines are
gentlefolk who abhor "a scene, " but are willing to fight for
what they believe in; and they are two old anvils who laugh at
broken hammers. In order to make clear how the battles in
the book are related to the opposing ideologies, it will be
necessary to study the structure of *The Old Wives' Tale,* book
by book.

I

The first book of *The Old Wives' Tale* could be called a
comedy of manners; the light tone Bennett maintains keeps
from being too monotonously evident the correspondence between the situations in which its heroine, Mrs. Baines, finds
herself, and those that confront her daughter Constance in
Books II and IV. Then, too, Bennett does not want to arouse
a great deal of sympathy for Mrs. Baines's plight, for this
would divert attention from Constance and Sophia, the girls
he is grooming for the book's protagonists. By treating Mrs.
Baines with an epigrammatic, Jane-Austenian condescension
which makes her almost a humor character, he keeps her two-
dimensional:

> The serious part of the dinner comprised roast
> beef and Yorkshire pudding--the pudding being
> served as a sweet course before the meat. Mrs.
> Baines ate freely of these things, for she loved
> them, and she was always hungry after a sermon.
> She also did well with the Cheshire cheese. Her
> intention was to sleep in the drawing-room after the
> repast. On Sunday afternoons she invariably tried
> to sleep in the drawing-room, and she did not often
> fail.

This is the offhand manner which Bennett adopts intentionally
to diminish Mrs. Baines. No wonder that, after such a prel-
ude, Samuel Povey's rude bursting in on the afternoon nap
to demand the hand of Constance does not herald the advent
of a tragedy. Bennett does not want it to, though it does herald
one of the major crises of the book--Mrs. Baines's decision
(and she is forced to reverse it) "that she and not Mr. Povey
should have ultimate rule over her house and shop."

Mrs. Baines's sister, the "widow from Axe," is treated
with still more wit and condescension: "No smoke at Axe! No
stuffiness at Axe! The spacious existence of a wealthy widow
in a residential town with a low death-rate and famous scen-
ery!" Harriet Maddack, "the widow from Axe," is, of the two
old wives in Book I, Sophia's counterpart. She recognizes her
spiritual daughter:

> Sophia was petted. Sophia was liable to be playfully
> tapped by Aunt Harriet's thimble when Aunt Harriet
> was hemming dusters (for the elderly lady could
> lift a duster to her own dignity). Sophia was called
> on two separate occasions, "My little butterfly."
> And Sophia was entrusted with the trimming of Aunt
> Harriet's new summer bonnet.

Very light and comic in tone, and yet a perfect parallel to
the situation in Book IV, in which old Constance and old Sophia
live together, is the unearthly alliance between mild Mother
Baines and stern Aunt Harriet: "The two vast widows shared
Mrs. Baines's bedroom, spending much of their time there

in long, hushed conversations--interviews from which Mrs.
Baines emerged with the air of one who has received enlightenment and Aunt Harriet with the air of one who has rendered
it. "

Even Mrs. Baines's final defeat at the end of Book I, a defeat which parallels Constance's near-defeat in Book IV, is
treated summarily, and yet remorselessly prepares the way
for Book IV's crucial struggle between Constance and Sophia:

> Mrs. Baines getting into the wagonette for Axe;
> Mrs. Baines, encumbered with trunks and parcels,
> leaving the scene of her struggles and her defeat,
> whither she had once come slim as a wand, to re-
> turn stout and heavy, and heavy-hearted, to her
> childhood; content to live with her grandiose sister
> until such time as she should be ready for burial.

But though Mrs. Baines thus ignominiously departs from
Book I, in seeming defeat, she is eventually to triumph. In
Book II we learn that she has outlived "her grandiose sister"
and in Book IV she posthumously triumphs in the twin victories of her disciple and daughter Constance; first in "the
buried question of domicile, " when Constance resists Sophia's
plans to uproot her from Bursley and transplant her to some
sophisticated version of the smokeless Axe, and second in
Constance's outliving, like Mrs. Baines, the more aggressive
sister, a victory which Constance herself is the first to ap-
preciate:

> Everybody considered that Constance had "come
> splendidly through" the dreadful affair of Sophia's
> death. Indeed, it was observed that she was more
> philosophic, more cheerful, more sweet, than she
> had been for many years. The truth was that, though
> her bereavement had been the cause of a most gen-
> uine and durable sorrow, it had been a relief to her.
> . . . Certainly Constance had fought Sophia on the
> main point, the question of domicile, and won; but
> . . . Sophia had been "too much" for Constance,
> and . . . the death of Mrs. Scales had put an end to

all the strain, and Constance had been once again
mistress in Constance's house.

Mrs. Baines, at the end of Book I, seems to have been defeated but eventually her defeats turn into triumphs. Constance
proves what her mother has not lived to prove, that there is
life in the Old Order yet.

What are the battles that prepare Mrs. Baines for her crucial defeat--the ousting from Bursley--at the end of Book I?
They will repay careful study, for they are the microcosm on
which the entire macrocosm of *The Old Wives' Tale* rests.
Mrs. Baines's antagonists are, then, two: her daughter Sophia
and Samuel Povey (Constance inherits both antagonists from
her mother, and they plague her throughout the remainder of
the book). As Sophia emerges in Book I seemingly the more
formidable and certainly the more engaging of the two enemies,
I shall first discuss her battles. Sophia fights twice in Book I,
both times against her mother. The first battle, paralleling
Edwin's in Book I of *Clayhanger,* is to choose a career which
will give her a chance for taste; the second is to choose a
husband who will give her Paris and all it symbolizes. She
wins, or seems to have won at the end of Book I, both battles.

For Sophia's is an early version of the Five Towns predicament; she is faced, in a simpler form, with the dual choice
that confronts Hilda Lessways. It is an enlightening experience
to witness the surprise and consternation of Mrs. Baines and
her daughter (and disciple) Constance, when apprised of Sophia's decision in the matter of her career:

> "Shut that door, " Mrs. Baines replied, pointing to
> the door which led to the passage; and while Con-
> stance obeyed, Mrs. Baines herself shut the stair-
> case-door. She then said, in a low, guarded voice--
>     "What's all this about Sophia wanting to be a
> school-teacher ?"
>     "Wanting to be a school-teacher ?" Constance re-
> peated, in tones of amazement.
>     "Yes. Hasn't she said anything to you ?"
>     "Not a word!"
>     "Well, I never! She wants to keep on with Miss

Chetwynd and be a teacher. " Mrs. Baines had half
a mind to add that Sophia had mentioned London.
But she restrained herself. There are some things
which one cannot bring oneself to say. She added,
"Instead of going into the shop!"

Here, Mrs. Baines and Constance have pretty well summed
up, between them, the crucial ingredients of a formidable
Bennett crisis, the crisis that faces Darius and his sister,
Mrs. Hamps, in Book I of *Clayhanger,* when Edwin defects.
The crisis is complex. First, there is the element of surprise, in Sophia's not wanting to go into the shop, not wanting to carry out the traditions of the still vigorous Baines
family; second, she chooses a profession which startles Mrs.
Baines and Constance, members of the commercial aristocracy; third, her ally is Miss Chetwynd, an *Old Wives' Tale*
version of the culture mediator; and fourth, there is an added
shock in Sophia's having "mentioned London." (Darius Clayhanger several times has to quell London in the breast of
Edwin; and Edwin himself, as inheritor of the printing business, has later to contend with similar urges in his foster son,
George Edwin. )

Sophia's reasons for doing battle are crucial to an understanding of the Five Towns predicament--she is unfitted for
life in commercial Bursley, like Edwin, who "had nothing in
him of the commercial traveler. " For Sophia "had always
hated the shop. She did not understand how her mother and
Constance could bring themselves to be deferential and flat-
tering to every customer that entered. . . . But long ago she
had decided that she would never go into the shop. "

Sophia has chosen so startlingly the career of school teacher, because the choices for a girl who did not want to "go into the shop" were extremely limited. "She knew that she would
be expected to do something, and she had fixed on teaching as
the one possibility. " More important, her choice is influenced
by the woman who acts as her substitute mother, Miss Chetwynd. Unfortunately Sophia's Miss Chetwynd is an old maid,
and a rather simpering creature in general; but there are the
familiar clues which mark her out as the substitute mother of
Sophia:

> Miss Chetwynd could choose ground from which
> to look down upon Mrs. Baines, who after all was
> in trade. Miss Chetwynd had no trace of the local
> accent; she spoke with a southern refinement which
> the Five Towns, while making fun of it, envied.
> . . . And she was the fount of etiquette, a won-
> der of correctness; in the eyes of her pupil's par-
> ents not so much "a perfect *lady*" as "a *perfect*
> lady. "

The phrase "no trace of the local accent" always heralds,
in Bennett, the entrance of the substitute parent and the culture mediator, and though Miss Chetwynd is a poor substitute
for Osmond Orgreave or even Tertius Ingpen, she is the best
that a Sophia Baines of "the Middle Ages, " daughter of a member of the "Aristocracy of the Square, " could contrive. And,
like all Bennett's parent substitutes, she has connections outside the Five Towns. Mrs. Baines is dashed to learn that
Miss Chetwynd's sister is to marry the Reverend Archibald
Jones, who "lived in London, and shot out into the provinces
at week-ends, preaching on Sundays and giving a lecture, *tinc-
tured with bookishness* [italics mine] 'in the chapel' on Mon-
day evenings. " For provincial Mrs. Baines, Mr. Jones is
invested with mystery, as indeed is his bride-to-be, "who
had left the Five Towns a quarter of a century before at the
age of twenty, " thus becoming a Bursley exile.
Miss Chetwynd is then, after all, a formidable substitute
mother, and she wins this battle for the soul of Sophia. But
not because of her pretensions to taste; the wife of John Baines
is not a woman to be cowed by that. Mrs. Baines yielded
(as her daughter Constance was to yield in the parallel decision that closes Book II, to permit her son Cyril his career as a London artist), not because she was impressed by
Miss Chetwynd, but because she recognized 'Sophia's complete inability to hear reason and wisdom. " Bennett's comments on Mrs. Baines's decision are significant of the strategic position this first decisive battle occupies in the whole
structure of *The Old Wives' Tale*: "There is no need to insist
on the tragic grandeur of Mrs. Baines's renunciation--a renunciation which implied her acceptance of a change in the

balance of power in her realm, " and again, " *'Then you think Sophia would make a good teacher?'* asked Mrs. Baines, and with a smile. But the words marked an epoch in her mind. All was over. "

And so Mrs. Baines is bested in the first crucial battle in *The Old Wives' Tale* (not counting a battle for Sam Povey's tooth, which, as I shall show when I discuss it later, is illustrative rather than functional). Sophia is to be apprenticed to Miss Chetwynd, and eventually to go to London, having won the battle that Edwin loses in Book I of *Clayhanger*. Significantly, however, Sophia gives up the dream of her career for the dream of Gerald Scales. Revealing is the scene in which, having renounced teaching so that she may see the commercial traveler when he visits the Baines shop, Sophia reflects:

> She had sacrificed her life for worse than nothing. She had made her own tragedy . . . exchanged content for misery and pride for humiliation--and with it all, Gerald Scales had vanished! She was ruined.
> She took to religion, and her conscientious Christian Virtues, practised with stern inclemency, were the canker of the family.

It is possible to underestimate the complexity of Bennett's structure in *The Old Wives' Tale*--not only possible, it has always been done. And, perhaps for that reason, no critic has realized that this renunciation of life, made before Sophia is at all intimately linked with Gerald Scales, deliberately parallels her final renunciation of Chirac in favor of the Pension Frensham, also because of Gerald's vanishing. But an understanding of Sophia's tendency to renounce is an essential clue to why, in her later years, Bennett describes her as "prim, " and why Constance thinks of Sophia's as a "wasted and sterile life. "

Her second battle with Mrs. Baines is, then, to gain possession of Gerald Scales. Why Sophia wants Gerald is a mystery unless her desire to rise to the next cultural level is understood, because, though naturally biology enters into her choice, in Bennett the biological instinct can be treated as negligible in his heroines' selection of a mate. (I shall take

up this question more fully in my discussion of *Hilda Lessways.*)

Sophia gives up the London career sponsored by Miss Chetwynd for Gerald Scales and the superior life of Paris. Gerald,
who seems to Sophia "the very symbol and incarnation of the
masculine and the elegant, " is "gentlemanly to a degree that
impressed her more than anything had impressed her in her
life. And all the proud and aristocratic instinct that was at the
base of her character sprang up and seized on his gentleman-
liness like a famished animal seizing on food. "

He is not only correct in his manners, and subtly aristocratic, but he has friends among the cultivated people of the
town:

> "I stayed in the town on purpose to go to a New
> Year's party at Mr. Lawton's, " Mr. Scales was
> saying.
> "Ah! So you know Lawyer Lawton!" observed
> Mrs. Baines, impressed, for Lawyer Lawton did
> not consort with tradespeople. He was jolly with
> them, and he did their legal business for them, but
> he was not of them. His friends came from afar.
> "My people are old acquaintances of his, " said
> Mr. Scales, sipping the milk which Maggie had
> brought. . . . It grew more and more evident that
> Mr. Scales, who went out to parties in evening
> dress, instead of going in respectable broadcloth
> to watch-night services, who knew the great ones
> of the land . . . was neither an ordinary commer-
> cial traveller nor the kind of man to which the Square
> was accustomed. He came from a different world.

His elegant worldliness helps Sophia to attain the sensation
she most desires, that of being set apart from the rest of provincial Bursley. Sophia and Gerald, while looking down at the
navvies toiling in the pits, experience an identical conviction
of their aristocracy:

> She and Gerald Scales glanced down at these dan-
> gerous beasts of prey in their yellow corduroys and

their open shirts revealing hairy chests. No doubt
they both thought how inconvenient it was that rail-
ways could not be brought into existence without the
aid of such revolting and swinish animals. They
glanced down from the height of their nice decorum
and felt the powerful attraction of similar superior
manners.

Gerald's ultimate worthiness is proved for Sophia, as George
Cannon's is for Hilda Lessways, by a discovery that he knows
France intimately: "And then, Paris! Paris meant absolutely
nothing to her but pure, impossible, unattainable romance.
And he had been there! The clouds of glory were around him."
And again: "She, living her humdrum life at the shop! And he,
elegant, brilliant, coming from far cities!"
The qualities that endear Gerald to Sophia make him distasteful to Mrs. Baines. Instinctively she recognizes in him
a threat to her balance of power. With the "formidable, thrice-
callous egotism of the provinces," she decides the affair must
be stopped. Already she has barely escaped one disastrous
defeat, in Sophia's abortive attempt to choose a career for
herself, and a second threatens in Constance's love for Samuel Povey, that menace to her dominion in the shop and the
home. In Gerald Scales she recognizes yet another impending battle: "Mr. Scales should have no finger in the pie of
*her* family." With Sophia's elopement, Mrs. Baines's struggles are at an end; at the close of Book I she rides off to Axe,
leaving to Constance and Books II and IV the task of reclaim-
ing Bursley for the Old Order.

## II

Book II develops two main battles, both waged by Constance
in the name of the Old Order, and both lost, but gallantly and,
as it were, triumphantly: her struggles to overcome her husband Samuel, the card, and her son Cyril, the artist. Samuel
Povey is one of the most misunderstood characters in *The
Old Wives' Tale.* Bennett treats him with such continual banter, that he obscures Povey's essential differences from Constance. In Book I, the "mild Constance" (in love) has eagerly

helped Povey with each new enterprise, her pliability dis-
guising that she and Samuel are not two slices from the same
loaf. Even in Book I, though, there are hints that Samuel is a
man of the future, an apostle both of progress and of taste.
His innovations in the shop, for example, incur the immediate
hostility of Mrs. Baines:

> Mr. Povey had recently been giving attention to
> the question of tickets. It is not too much to say that
> Mr. Povey, to whom heaven had granted a minimum
> share of imagination, had nevertheless discovered
> his little parcel of imagination in the recesses of
> being, and brought it effectively to bear on tickets.
> Tickets ran in conventional grooves. . . . He
> dreamed of other tickets, in original shapes, with
> original legends. In brief, he achieved, in regard
> to tickets, the rare feat of ridding himself of pre-
> conceived notions, and of approaching a subject with
> fresh, virginal eyes. . . .
> And did Mrs. Baines encourage him in his sin-
> gle-minded enterprise on behalf of *her* business ?
> Not a bit! Mrs. Baines's attitude, when not disdain-
> ful, was inimical! . . . And every few days Mr.
> Povey thought of some new and wonderful word to
> put on a ticket.
> His last miracle was the word "exquisite."

This use of the word "exquisite" sums Povey up as a man of
the New Order, as it sums Mr. Orgreave up for Edwin, in
*Clayhanger*. And Mrs. Baines is right in her instinctive distrust of such a word from such a man: "'exquisite' written
upon a window-ticket! No! What would John Baines have thought
of 'exquisite'!"
Whenever "the chasm" opens between Constance and Samuel
during their married life, a difference in ideologies causes
the rift. The first marked difference occurs because Constance,
daughter of the commercial aristocracy, says to Samuel: "You
surely aren't going to begin wearing those horrid paper collars
again!" All the differences in Constance and Samuel are implicit in that question: she comes from the class that believes

in clothes that are unostentatiously good. (When, an old woman,
she meets after thirty years the smart Sophia at the railroad
station, she reflects that Sophia's clothes are a little loud.)
In wearing paper collars Samuel offends everything that is
Baines in Constance, and in such an affair he is bound to come
off second best. For, as Sophia reflects when, an old exile,
she receives her first letter from forgiving Constance:

> Constance personified for her the qualities of the
> Baines family. Constance's letter was a great let-
> ter . . . the natural expression of the Baines char-
> acter at its best. Not an awkward reference in the
> whole of it! No clumsy expression of surprise at
> anything that she, Sophia, had done, or failed to do!
> . . . Just a sublime acceptance of the situation as
> it was, and the assurance of undiminished love.
> . . .

The Baineses are an old family compared to that of Samuel
Povey, and Bennett often suggests that, both in the matter of
paper collars and of tactful letters, they could teach Povey a
thing or two.

Another hint that Mr. Povey is not the man for Constance
is his approval of Gerald Scales's values, particularly in the
importance of owning hunting dogs. In his role of man of the
world, Povey is interested in Scales as dog fancier, and when
he is safely married to Constance, begins to sail boldly under
his true colors. And not only dogs are part of his appurte-
nances, but--defiance to the shade of Mr. Baines--cigars.
In every way, to the best of his small bent, he fulfills that
picture of the landed gentry which the "Death of Simon Fuge"
centers in Mr. Brindley. When Samuel says openly to hor-
rified Constance, "I think I'll have a weed!" he comes out,
says Bennett, "in his true colours as a blood, a blade, and a
gay spark."

These small touches which distinguish Samuel the Card from
Conservator Constance prepare for the final battle between
husband and wife--Samuel's championship of his cousin, Daniel
Povey. This battle, resulting in the first crucial defeat for
Constance in Book II, is caused by Samuel's identifying him-

self with Daniel so completely that he gives up all concern
for his own and his family's welfare. Samuel idolizes Daniel
because his cousin represents all that he would like to be:

> Everyone liked Daniel Povey; he was a favourite
> among all ranks. . . . He had dignity without the
> slightest stiffness; he was welcomed by his equals
> and frankly adored by his inferiors. . . . He was
> one of the remnant who had kept alive the great
> Pan tradition from the days of the Regency through
> the vast, arid Victorian expanse of years. . . .
> If it did not explain his friendship with the rector
> of St. Luke's, it explained his departure from the
> Primitive Methodist connexion, to which the Poveys
> as a family had belonged since Primitive Method-
> ism was created in Turnhill in 1807. . . . Samuel
> gazed upwards at the handsome long nose and rich
> lips of his elder cousin, so experienced, so agree-
> able, so renowned, so esteemed, so philosophic,
> and admitted to himself that he had lived to the age
> of forty in a state of comparative boobyism.

Because of this idolatry, when Daniel was on trial for killing
his worthless wife, Samuel "lived solely for Daniel's trial,
pouring out money in preparation for it . . . he took the enterprise upon himself, to the neglect of his business and the scorn
of his health." And he "became Daniel's defending angel, rescuing Daniel from Daniel's own weakness and apathy. He became, indeed, Daniel."

This preoccupation of Samuel's with the defense of his cousin brings him into direct and crucial conflict with Constance.
The first of two decisive battles in the second book, it shows
the "mild Constance" in an entirely new light, important to an
understanding of *The Old Wives' Tale*'s theme:

> It was a battle between her will and his that occurred
> one night when Constance, marshalling all her for-
> ces, suddenly insisted that he must go out no more
> until he was cured of his persistent cough. She de-
> liberately gave way to hysteria; she was no longer

soft and gentle; she flung bitterness at him like vit-
riol; she shrieked like a common shrew. It seems
almost incredible that Constance should have gone
so far; but she did. She accused him, amid sobs,
of putting his cousin before his wife and son. . . .
It was a most extraordinary scene, and quite unique
in their annals. Constance was beaten. She accepted
defeat, gradually controlling her sobs and changing
her tone to the tone of the vanquished. She kissed
him in bed, kissing the rod. And he gravely kissed
her.

When Daniel is condemned to death, Samuel even tries to
provide some link between Daniel and the future by taking Cyril
to see him in his cell; of course this meets with further opposition from Constance:

She would only admit that the case had "got on" his
mind. A startling proof of this was that he actually
suggested taking Cyril with him to see the condemned man. He wished Cyril to see Daniel; he said
gravely that he thought Cyril ought to see him. The
proposal was monstrous, inexplicable--or explicable
only by the assumption that his mind, while not un-
hinged, had temporarily lost its balance. Constance
opposed an absolute negative, and Samuel being in
every way enfeebled she overcame.

This victory which saves Cyril from Daniel is the crisis in
the battle between Constance and Samuel. His death, caused
by exposure while trying to get a pardon for Daniel, is in a
way a triumph for Constance, though of course she is too good-
hearted to take it as such.

Constance's second battle--with Cyril--is the inevitable corollary of Samuel Povey's death, as she immediately turns to
him as husband-substitute. During lulls in her struggle with
Samuel, Cyril's unfitness to be her second mate has been made
clear. (Since the influence of sex on Bennett's heroines is
seemingly negligible, Constance's involvement with Cyril can
be taken as her second, and with Sophia as her third, mar-

riage.) No mate could be more unsuited to Conservator Constance than Cyril, the dilettante. (The dilettante is one extreme
of Bennett's architect; as culture-hobbyist Edwin is the other.)

As long as Samuel lives, Constance's position as mediator
between him and his son obscures the essential differences between her and Cyril. (The Samuel-Cyril clash parallels in
kind though not in development the Darius-Clayhanger clash.)
Constance shields the boy from consequences of his steal-
ing--as Aunt Harriet has shielded his mother-substitute, So-
phia--and from the Baines-Povey pattern, her position paralleling Mrs. Baines's stand in regard to Sophia:

> She could not change Samuel; besides, he was right!
> And though Cyril was not yet five, she felt that she
> could not change Cyril either. He was just as un-
> changeable as a growing plant. The thought of her
> mother and Sophia did not present itself to her; she
> felt, however, somewhat as Mrs. Baines had felt
> on historic occasions; but, being more softly kind,
> younger, and less chafed by destiny, she was con-
> scious of no bitterness, conscious rather of a sol-
> emn blessedness.

Art, the field of argument between Edwin and Darius Clayhanger, is the chief cause of the parent-son battles in Book II
of *The Old Wives' Tale,* for though consciously Samuel and
Constance are willing for Cyril to become an artist, unconsciously they are opposed to his doing so. This subterranean
opposition is manifest in Samuel's tossing Cyril's water color
into the fire, in punishment for the boy's having stolen money
for cigarettes: "And he pitched into the fire--not the apparatus
of crime, but the water-colour drawing of a moss-rose and
the straws and the blue ribbon for bows at the corners."

The final triumph of artist over card and conservator is
prepared for by Bennett's emphasis on Cyril's first decisive
victory, which is at the end of a chapter, and parallels the
Sophia-Constance clash in Book IV, "Towards Hotel Life":

> When he first said: "I say, mother, why can't we
> go to Llandudno instead of Buxton this year?" his

mother thought he was out of his senses. For the
idea of going to any place other than Buxton was in-
conceivable! Had they not always been to Buxton?
What would their landlady sày? How could they ever
look her in the face again? Besides. . . well . . .!
They went to Llandudno, rather scared, and hardly
knowing how the change had come about. But they
went. And it was the force of Cyril's will, Cyril the
theoretic cipher, that took them.

Having by many such touches built up the clash between
mother and son, while still permitting the parents' own battle
to carry the main action, Bennett is able, at Samuel's death,
to assume the essential Cyril-Constance differences, and begin immediately at the heart of the battle. With such small
crises as Cyril's forgetting to come home to tea--the one
ceremony Constance had symbolized as a sort of love feast for
her and her son, Bennett through a series of scenes and in-
terpolations builds to the implied conclusion that Cyril does
not regard Constance as his mother in any real sense. Their
ideologies are too different. Like Edwin Clayhanger, he turns
from the parent to the substitute parent--in Book II, Matthew
Peel-Swynnerton, cultured Five Townsman with roots in London and Paris, and in Book IV to his Aunt Sophia.
    The decisive, though not the final, skirmish occurs in Cyr-
il's decision to go to evening classes at the School of Art. Constance opposes this move for a double reason: "His father had
decided absolutely against the project, " and, though Samuel
is now dead, for a reason of her own: "three solitary evenings
a week, waiting for him to come home. " But when she "hints
that if he attends the School of Art she would be condemned to
solitary evenings, he looks at her as though saying: 'Well, and
if you are--?'" In denying that his duty to his mother is superior to his duty to art, he is "the image of his Aunt Sophia. "
Cyril's victory, given Constance's temperament and his own,
is never in doubt: "She said to herself: 'If we can be happy together only when I give way to him, I must give way to him. '
And there was ecstasy in her yielding. "
    A double defeat for Constance closes Book II: at the same
time that Cyril, ornament of her life, is awarded the National

Scholarship which means his eventual exile, the historic
Baines shop is bought from Constance by Mr. Critchlow, the
evil genius of the decaying Old Order. Although Constance remains stubbornly rooted in her domicile, merely bricking up
the walls between the house and the shop, "in the future she
would be compelled, if she wished to enter the shop, to enter
it as a customer and from the front. Yes, she saw that, though
the house remained hers, the root of her life had been wrenched
up." (But her triumph over Sophia's attempt to wrench her
from her roots is her first important victory in Book IV.)

After such a disaster, Cyril's final flitting to London, inevitable from the moment his mother yields to him in the matter of art classes at night, might have been anticlimax. Nevertheless it figures as the final and the decisive defeat of Book
II, and Constance recognizes it as major.

> With what futile and bitter execration she mur-
> mured in her heart the word "If." If Cyril's child-
> ish predilections had not been encouraged! If he had
> only been content to follow in his father's trade!
> If she had flatly refused to sign his indenture at
> Peel's and pay the premium! If he had not turned
> from colour to clay! If the art-master had not had
> that fatal "idea"! If the judges for the competition
> had decided otherwise! If only she had brought Cyril
> up in habits of obedience, sacrificing temporary
> peace to permanent security!

The crisis is made all the more painful for Constance by the
irony that *she* must *choose* whether he goes to London or not--
since he is a minor, he cannot go without her consent; furthermore, "he would want a lot more money, which he could ob-
tain from none but her." Constance's difficulty is like Christopher Newman's, who fails to purchase his countess; she has
the money but she cannot buy the one thing she wants--sophis-
ticated, artistic Cyril, the ornament of her old age. And even
the good manners she inherited from generations of commercial aristocrats are against her: "No! she could not refuse.
He was the master, the tyrant. For the sake of daily pleasant-
ness she had weakly yielded to him at the start!"

Of Constance's two major defeats in Book II, this is the more decisive, though it is less actively contested. Constance thinks, "I'm a lonely old woman now. I've nothing to live for anymore, and I'm no use to anybody." Unconsciously, she is preparing herself for her third ill-mated marriage--to Sophia.

## III

Book III presents Sophia's awakening, in Paris, to the realization that Gerald Scales is not "the very symbol and incarnation of the masculine and the elegant, " but a fool without manners, who "could not be relied upon not to make himself and her ridiculous, tragically ridiculous. " Here are the beginnings of her long retreat from the dreamed-of values of Paris to the small haven of Bursley. Book I has prepared us for Sophia's retreat, by showing how she "took to religion" when Gerald Scales disappointed her the first time.

Sophia ceases to love Gerald when she finds he is completely lacking in taste. Gerald had been a mediator for Sophia, between Bursley and Paris, but in Paris she meets two men who show him up as a shoddy imitation: a rather disagreeable Englishman, who "evidently belonged to a much higher rank than Gerald's, " and who succeeds in making Gerald appear, to Sophia, a provincial boor; and Chirac, a Frenchman--formerly an architect--whose "manners were more wonderful than any that Sophia had ever imagined. " In two crucial scenes, the supper at the Restaurant Sylvain, and the execution at Auxterre, Bennett makes explicit Sophia's reasons for ceasing to love Gerald.

The scene in the Restaurant Sylvain presents Gerald as a Bursley boor confronted by the superior manners of the English aristocracy, and shows Sophia that "while seeking to impress the Englishman, he was merely becoming ridiculous to the Englishman. " It presents Gerald to Sophia three-dimensionally, against a background which throws the shadowed parts of his portrait into relief; she sees him now not as the adored son of a wealthy and distinguished commercial line, but as a member of the *nouveau riche,* a man with the millionaire's problem but without the saving degree of awareness and humility:

Gerald, though he could always comfort himself by
the thought that he had been to a university with the
best, felt his own inferiority and could not hide that
he felt it. Gerald was wealthy; he came of a wealthy
family; but he had not the habit of wealth. When he
spent money furiously, he did it with bravado, too
conscious of grandeur and too conscious of the difficulties of acquiring that which he threw away.

Gerald's futile attempt to impress the aristocratic Englishman "slightly lowered him in her esteem, " but her next, and
crucial, disillusionment some half hour later shows her a
Gerald blind to the demand of manners, deserting her in the
restaurant to engage in a drunken brawl. She then first realizes fully her crucial error in judgment and foresees in Gerald's entire lack of taste the ruin of their marriage:

> She felt like an indiscreet little girl, and she looked
> like one. No youthful radiant beauty of features, no
> grace and style of a Parisian dress, no certificate
> of a ring, no premature initiation into the mysteries,
> could save her from the appearance of a raw fool
> whose foolishness had been her undoing.

In rescuing her from the precarious social position as a
solitary woman in a restaurant, Chirac only serves to give
her a second model to measure Gerald against, and to make
her realize fully for the first time that her choice of Gerald
as a road to Paris has been (as Hilda Lessways' choice of
George Cannon is) tragically foolish: "Compare him with Mr.
Chirac. She leaned despairingly on the table. She would not
undress. She would not move. She had to realize her position;
she had to see it. " (This early introduction of Chirac as a culture mediator for Sophia is significant, for later he is the man
she rejects, and in doing so rejects the culture of Paris for
Bursley values in a Paris boarding house. )
The execution scene at Auxterre makes clear that Sophia is
not ready for Paris. Though she is attracted by the superior
Chirac, she does not have the instinct for experience demanded
for such an outing as an execution, an instinct personified in

Chirac, the architect-newspaperman; nor does she have the lust for experience personified in Gerald, which makes such outings as the Bursley picnic for a dead elephant, or the Paris excursion to watch a man guillotined, equally palatable. (The chapter in Book I, "Elephant, " presents deliberately a preparatory parallel to the execution at Auxterre.) She is puzzled by Chirac's intense and yet impersonal interest in his own reactions to the execution--what Bennett describes, in *Clayhanger,* as "the impartial and unmoved spectator . . . in everybody who possesses artistic sensibility, watching his secret life as from a conning-tower." Sophia's lack of impersonal curiosity shows up sharply in Paris, but not for the first time; in Bursley she had displayed the same indifference toward the promise of a dead elepahnt. And now:

> "As psychological experience," replied Chirac, pronouncing the *p* of the adjective, "it will be very *interessant* . . . to observe one's self, in such circumstances. . . ." He smiled enthusiastically.
>      She thought how strange even nice Frenchmen were. Imagine going to an execution in order to observe yourself!

Gerald's more primitive approach to the execution is even more distasteful to Sophia than Chirac's:

> As the dinner finished, Gerald's pose of a calm, disinterested scientific observer of humanity gradually broke down . . . his restless glance carefully avoided both Sophia and Chirac. The latter, whose unaffected simplicity of interest in the affair had more than anything helped to keep Sophia in countenance, observed . . . Sophia's excessive discomfort, and suggested that they should leave the table. . . .

The greed for raw experience which Gerald displays at the execution of Rivain, plus his lack of a stomach strong enough to digest the experience, causes the third disillusionment that finally destroys Sophia's remaining love for Gerald:

Gerald staggered past her into the room and sank
with a groan on to the bed. Not long since he had
been proudly conversing with impudent women. Now,
in a swift collapse, he was as flaccid as a sick hound
and as disgusting as an aged drunkard. . . .
   This was what he had brought her to, then! The
horrors of the night, of the dawn, and of the morning! Ineffable suffering and humiliation; anguish
and torture that could never be forgotten! And after a fatuous vigil of unguessed license, he had tot-
tered back, an offensive beast, to sleep the day away
in that filthy chamber! *He did not possess even
enough spirit to play the role of roysterer to the end.*
[Italics mine. ] Such was her brilliant and godlike
husband, the man who had given her the right to call
herself a married woman! He was a fool.

Sophia stays with him until he deserts her four years later,
but only because, with Baines pride, she is ashamed to confess to Bursley that she has mistaken a minor commercial
traveler for a man of taste.
Sophia has misjudged both herself and experience. The description of the execution is crucial to an understanding of this
theme which conditions the rest of Sophia's career.

   And Sophia waited, horrorstruck. She saw nothing
but the gleaming triangle of metal that was suspend-
ed high above the prone, attendant victim. She felt
like a lost soul, torn too soon from shelter, and ex-
posed forever to the worst hazards of destiny. Why
was she in this strange, incomprehensible town, foreign and inimical to her, watching with agonized
glance this cruel, obscene spectacle? Her sensibilities were all a bleeding mass of wounds. Why?
Only yesterday, and she had been an innocent, timid creature in Bursley, in Axe, a foolish creature
who deemed the concealment of letters a supreme
excitement. Either that day or this day was not
real. Why was she imprisoned alone in that odious

> hotel, with no one to soothe and comfort her, and
> carry her away?
>     The distant bell boomed once. Then a monosyllab-
> ic voice sounded, sharp, low, nervous; she recog-
> nized the voice of the executioner, whose name she
> had heard but could not remember. There was a
> clicking noise . . .
>     She shrank down to the floor in terror and loath-
> ing, and hid her face, and shuddered.

Witnessing the execution of Rivain, her sensibilities "all a
bleeding mass of wounds, " leaves Sophia with an instinct for
experience impaired, and with a determination that she will
never again become involved. Like Philip in Graham Greene's
"The Basement Room, " too early an introduction to experience
makes the rest of Sophia's life in Paris one long retreat from
involvement. She will not allow herself even the luxurious emotion of gratitude toward the courtesans who save her life when,
deserted by Gerald, she lies dying of fever in the Paris streets.
She prefers to pay the courtesans well for having worked un-
selfishly to save her, though they beg for her gratitude.
    Bennett feels that Sophia had greater potentialities than Con-
stance--*The Old Wives' Tale* demonstrates that conviction
again and again--but he implies that in her retreat from life
the values of Bursley unfit her for the values of Paris, as the
latter unfit her for a return to the provinces. Therefore she
involves herself in her work as boardinghouse keeper, work
which she feels she can trust because she is responsible to
no one but herself, and because she can apply to it the standards of Bursley. Bennett shows her becoming almost a miser,
a recluse, living in the Paris which should have been so uniquely her home: "She was making money, and she wanted to make
more. She was always inventing ways of economy. She was so
anxious to achieve independence that money was always in her
mind. She began to love gold, to love hoarding it, and to hate
paying it away. . . ."
    But life gives Sophia a second chance to satisfy the "in-
stinct for experience"; Chirac, the newspaperman and ex-
architect, wants Sophia. Sophia will not have him. Not because he does not attract her physically:

It was infinitely sweet to her, voluptuously sweet,
this basking in the heat of temptation. It certainly
did seem to her, then, the one real pleasure in the
world. Her body might have been saying to his:
"Look into my mind. For you I have no modesty.
Look and see all that is there." The veil of convention seemed to have been rent. Their attitude to each
other was almost that of lover and mistress . . .
morally she was his mistress in that moment.

Not because he is not, in many ways, what she has always desired in a man, what she was looking for in Gerald Scales.
What is wrong with Chirac is a very positive, rather than a
negative thing: he cares too much about Sophia: "She continued to dream, at rare intervals, of the kind of passion that
would have satisfied her, glowing but banked down like a fire
in some fine chamber of a rich but careful household." Like
the little boy in "The Basement Room," she is through with involving herself in the lives of others:

"I cannot be bothered with all that sort of thing. It
is not worth while. What does it lead to? Is not life
complicated enough without that? No, no! I will stay
as I am. At any rate I know what I am in for, as
things are!" And she would reflect upon her hopeful
financial situation.

*Riceyman Steps* makes clear Bennett's attitude toward the
miser. His condemnation of Sophia's gradually growing ascet-
icism practiced in the name of money is equally unsparing,
and explains why he permits Constance to have the last word
on Sophia's "wasted and sterile life." Although he devotes an
entire book of *The Old Wives' Tale* to what he considers Constance's meaningful and rich life in Bursley, five pages suf-
fice him after Sophia rejects Chirac. "This was the end of
Sophia's romantic adventures in France. . . . For Sophia the
conclusion of the siege meant chiefly that prices went down."
The last five pages present an increasingly unpleasant portrait of a Sophia "employing two servants, working them very
hard at low wages," a Sophia "who has acquired the landlady's

manner, " and who, with typical Bennett symbolism, is "known
as Mrs. Frensham. Across the balconies of two windows the
Frenshams had left a gilded sign, 'Pension Frensham,' and
Sophia had not removed it. " Thus she loses even the symbol
of her identity. It is this Mrs. Frensham, a woman who has
"forgotten the face of love," who is "*the* landlady: efficient,
stylish, diplomatic, and tremendously experienced," that Bennett brings back to Bursley, involved at last, caught by the
mild Constance in a marriage unsuited not only to Mrs. Frensham of Paris, but to the original Sophia Baines.

## IV

Book IV of *The Old Wives' Tale* reveals Constance Baines
as the heroine of the Old Order, in all the triumphant meek-
ness of two victorious battles. It has become an established
convention of Bennett criticism to call Time the hero of *The
Old Wives' Tale*; Time is not even the villain, because in this
praise of the will, "what life is" is the important secret, and
time does not prevent Constance from penetrating it. Once she
has done so, she is ready to die: "the invincible common-
sense of a sound nature prevented her . . . from feebly dis-
solving in self-pity. . . . She had tasted triumphant hours.
. . . No one but Constance could realize all that Constance
had been through, and all that life had meant to her. " But
Sophia does not know what life is, though she has had immense
experience: "it was the riddle of life that was puzzling and
killing her. "

By obvious standards Sophia has lived a fuller life than Constance. Married at eighteen in an elopement to London and Paris, she spends half her life in the capital of France and returns, a rich and fabulous revenant, to confound the provin-
cials who have prophesied her ruin. But Constance does not
think Sophia has lived more fully than she, and neither does
Bennett, though Constance spends her sixty-odd years growing fat and fussy in a province in the exact geographical center of England.

For Constance has fulfilled her potentialities. If she is
"rather a fragile, small, fat woman, soon out of breath, easily tired, " she had always promised to be one, and she is still

uniquely a Baines, "the very spirit of simple love, " of whom
a sophisticated and successful Parisian can still say, "Constance! At that moment there was assuredly for Sophia no
creature in the world like Constance. Constance personified
for her the qualities of the Baines family . . . the natural ex-
pression of the Baines character at its best. " And yet she is
withal a dangerous enemy and an even more dangerous friend,
who can best an aristocrat like Matthew Peel-Swynnerton: "She
would pay the cabman. Never before had Matthew permitted
a woman to pay for a cab in which he had ridden; but there
was no arguing with Constance. Constance was dangerous. "

It is the dangerous Constance who reaches out from Bursley
to capture Sophia from Paris, from the Rue Lord Byron, though
Sophia is "attached to it by the heavy chains of habit"; and it
is Constance's unique triumph that Sophia must come to Bursley for love of her, though she will not move from Bursley for
love of Sophia. At last, after half a century of nodding to the
will of others--after union with a card like Samuel and to an
artist like Cyril--"the mild Constance" succeeds in capturing
a mate in some ways more formidable than either, and in drag-
ging her back to chafe in a Bursley grown too small--and all
for love of her. Symbolic of Constance's victory is the unhappy
predicament of Fossette, Sophia's Parisian dog, who endures
the slings of Bursley along with her unhappy but involved mistress. Even the Bursley servants make unfair discriminations
against Fossette and in favor of Constance's dog Spot, and
Fossette must endure them all while she and Sophia remain
chained by Constance.

Book IV restates the themes which were iterated in Book I,
and gives them new meanings by reversing Mrs. Baines's defeat into Constance's triumph. Even the mother's removal to
Axe by her rich and confident sister is reversed: in Book IV
the sister comes from Paris, and though, like her Aunt Harriet, she finds Bursley "paltry, confined, and dull, " and
though, in what ends in being one of two crucial triumphs for
Constance, she plans to free Constance from Bursley and
take her to a continental version of the smokeless Axe (where
they could live out their lives, as their mother and aunt had
done, with Constance "having the air of one who has received
enlightenment, " and Sophia "the air of one who has rendered

it"), she is surprised to find that Constance's will is stronger than her own, and that, as Bennett says of the antifederation victory, Constance's second triumph, "the mere blind, deaf, inert forces of reaction, with faulty organization, and quite deprived of the aid of logic, had proved far stronger than all the alert enthusiasm arrayed against them. "

In winning her first big battle of Book IV--the first she has ever won--Constance employs different techniques from those she used in the battle she had lost to Samuel Povey. And this time, in being uniquely Constance, "absolutely wrong, " she "stuck to her ideas like a mule"; having "not argued at all, " she is stronger than the more enlightened widow:

> Sophia remembered the very words, "You can't alter her, " which she had used in remonstrating with Cyril. And now she had been guilty of precisely the same unreason as that with which she had reproached Cyril! She was ashamed, both for herself and for Constance. Assuredly it had not been such a scene as women of their age would want to go through often. It was humiliating. She wished that it could have been blotted out as though it had never happened. Neither of them ever forgot it. They had had a lesson. And particularly Sophia had had a lesson. Having learnt, they left for the Rutland, amid due ceremonies, and returned to St. Luke's Square.

This, Constance's first battle, reveals her strength as nothing has before revealed it. She is the woman who, while consciously longing for her son's affection, would not (as Dr. Stirling tells Sophia) "even hear of going to live in London with her beloved son. " Having lived more fully, she is able to do without Sophia better than Sophia is able to do without her: "She [Sophia] marvelled that a woman of Constance's sweet and calm disposition should be capable of so vast and ruthless an egotism. Constance must have known that Sophia would not leave her, and that the habitation of the Square was a continual irk to Sophia. " More than "a continual irk, " the Square ends in spoiling the nine remaining years of Sophia's life, which she spends in futile brooding: "After all it was scarcely conceivable that they should be living in the very middle of a dirty, ugly, industrial town simply because Constance mulishly declined to move. "

After Sophia's death, which Constance and Gerald by their claims for affection accomplish between them, Constance is "more philosophic, more cheerful, more sweet, than she had been for many years, " having "fought Sophia on the main point, and won. "

Sophia's two attacks of paralysis become symbolic of her major conflicts. The first attack comes when she suspects, from the attitude of Matthew Peel-Swynnerton, that he has recognized her and means to write Constance, involving Sophia again in the love for others which she has renounced in favor of the Pension Frensham:

> The vision of any change in her existence was in
> highest degree painful to her. And not only pain-
> ful! It frightened her. It made her shrink. But she
> could not dismiss it. . . . While dawn announced
> itself, slowly discovering each object in the cham-
> ber, she was ill. Fever seemed to rage in her head.
> And in and round her mouth she had strange sensa-
> tions. . . .

When, after a night of paralysis, the doctor prescribes ab-solute rest, "she marvelled that a few words with a man who chanced to be named Peel-Swynnerton could have resulted in such a disaster. "

The threat of having to love her sister Constance brings on her first attack of paralysis; her renewed involvement with Gerald, when she is summoned by telegram to his deathbed, brings on her second and fatal attack--so rigidly does Sophia resist love. She realizes then that, since the first four years of her marriage spent with Gerald, her life has been mean-ingless:

> He and she had once loved and burned and quarrelled
> in the glittering and scornful pride of youth. But
> time had worn them out. "Yet a little while, " she
> thought, "and I shall be lying on a bed like that! And

what shall I have lived for? What is the meaning of
it?" The riddle of life itself was killing her, and she
seemed to drown in a sea of inexpressible sorrow.

And standing by the dead body of her husband, she thinks of the
second chance life gave her, with Chirac: "She saw Chirac with
his wistful smile. She saw him whipped over the roof of the
Gare du Nord at the tail of a balloon. . . . Could she excite
lust now? Ah! the irony of such a question! To be young and
seductive, to be able to kindle a man's eye--that seemed to her
the sole thing desirable." On the way home, in the motor car
with the two young lovers who have what she now sees she
should have wanted, she has her fatal attack, bizarre in its
impact: "Lily could feel the poor old lady's heart."

A second, and equally important, part of Sophia's tragedy
is that she has not fulfilled the cultural potentialities of her
youth, the hopes of her substitute mother, Miss Chetwynd:
"In some ways I look on Sophia as the most remarkable girl
. . . that I have ever met with." (Sophia's problem is that of
Edwin Clayhanger, who also did not fulfill his promise, except that hers is the added burden of knowing it is her own
fault.) This realization of lost youth comes to her through Dr.
Stirling, who figures as culture mediator in several stories
of the Five Towns. She realizes that though the doctor assumes a residence in France includes a knowledge of French
literature, she "had read practically nothing since 1870; for
her the latest author was Cherbuliez." This, from a woman
who in her girlhood had formed, with Miss Chetwynd, "an aristocracy of the intellect"!

Her second cultural humbling comes in having to confess to
the élite of the Hotel Rutland that she does not know what is
going on at the Comédie Française, that she had not been inside a French theater in thirty years, and that she does not
know the English chaplain in Paris.

Furthermore, she learns that she has lived all the years of
her life without learning how to live; though she is a Parisian
hers is the Five Towns' version of the millionaire's predicament, for "Never could she spend her income! She did not
know how to spend it." Bennett explicitly recognizes her plight
in commenting, "And she could not, in her age, devise expen-

sive tastes. " Because she had always resisted involvement, because she is, as she now sees, "too free, too exempt from responsibilities, " she realizes that "if thirty thousand pounds or so could have bought a son like Cyril, she would have bought one for herself. "

But Sophia has not entirely failed to realize her potentialities. She is able to attract and hold the respect of taste mediators such as Dr. Stirling; and she wins over Constance in the battle for Cyril's filial affection. Constance early recognizes the threat to her security, in the likeness between Cyril and Sophia: "as a baby he was very like you. He was a handsome baby. " When she finds that, although she herself has not been able to coax Cyril down from redoubtable London, Sophia can do it with a word, she thinks: "Sophia, then, could do more with Cyril than she could! Sophia had only met him once, and could simply twist him around her little finger. " When Sophia, with her immense worldly knowledge--a quality which, since Bennett himself respected it highly, is not to be discounted--undertakes to reprimand Cyril for disrespect to his mother, she "was pleased with the way in which he had accepted her criticism, and the gesture with which he threw away the cigar-end struck her as very distinguished. "

Perhaps Sophia's greatest victory in Book IV is this capture of Constance's son, through the very values which, during the hard years in Paris, she had often regretted--thinking longingly of Bursley:

> The figure of Constance filled the doorway. Her
> face was troubled. She had heard Cyril in the street,
> and had come down to see why he remained so long
> in the parlour. She was astounded to find Sophia with
> him. There they were, intimate as cronies, chat-
> tering about Paris! Undoubtedly she was jealous!
> Never did Cyril talk like that to her!

Sophia's charm for Cyril and Peel-Swynnerton is that she has, in one sense, lived, even if not in the sense that she was capable of:

> Her eyes announced that she had lived and learnt,

that she knew more about life than any one whom
she was likely to meet, and that having pre-eminently succeeded in life, she had tremendous confidence in herself. The proof of her success was the
unique Frensham's. A consciousness of the uniqueness of Frensham's was also in those eyes.

But even in the matter of Frensham's uniqueness, Bennett
does not allow Sophia the last word; in the Rutland Hotel he
forces her to adjust her perspective and shows that her pride,
in its way, had been as provincial as Constance's conviction
of the superiority of St. Luke's Square: "To the eye the interior of the Rutland presented a spectacle far richer than the
Pension Frensham could show. The standard of comfort was
higher. The guests had a more distinguished appearance. It is
true that the prices were much higher. Sophia was humbled.
She had enough sense to adjust her perspective." Constance,
who does not have the sense to adjust her perspective, is, however, the stronger precisely for her pig-headedness, and it is
this provinciality which enables her to triumph over Sophia's
plan to uproot her, with a defiant, piteous, "There's some
of us like Bursley, black as it is!"
Cyril remains Sophia's unique triumph in Book IV, even at
the funerals of Sophia and Constance. For his Aunt Sophia's
funeral the usually tardy Cyril arrives on time, and immediately takes charge of everything:

Constance was afraid lest Cyril, despite the seri-
ousness of the occasion, might exhibit his custom-
ary tardiness in coming. She had long since learnt
not to rely on him. But he came the same evening.
His behaviour was in every way perfect. He showed
quiet but genuine grief for the death of his aunt. . . .
Further, he at once assumed charge of all arrange-
ments, in regard to both Sophia and her husband.
. . . He said, indeed, that he had never directed
anything before.

Recognizing him as her true son, Sophia has left him her entire
fortune, but he displays the artist's indifference to money; this

hurts his mother, who feels that "for the sake of Bursley, he
might have affected a little satisfaction, " but Sophia has had
his unbought affection, and she has been entirely satisfied.

Cyril is not at the funeral of Constance--"He arrived three
days later"--and there is irony in Constance's excusing him
as she lies dying: "If it was serious, " she said, "he would not
lose a moment. "

Constance's second battle and triumph in Book IV parallels
Samuel Povey's battle for and martyrdom to the New Order.
In her last years Constance finds a daughter-substitute in Lily
Holl, Dick Povey's fiancée. For Lily Holl, "a nice, quiet, la-
dylike girl, " is the child of Constance's age, daughter to her
in the real sense that Cyril has never been son. (Cyril's de-
priving Lily and Dick of their promised wedding present from
Constance after the old lady's death, is Bennett's usual precise
symbolizing.) Constance explicitly recognizes her relationship
with Lily, by giving the substitute-daughter a fine cameo brooch
that has belonged to her own mother.

The test of Lily's discipleship, however, comes in her en-
gagement to Dick Povey, who is the direct inheritor of Samuel's
and Daniel's cardishness. (In Book II this final symbolism is
prepared for by scenes in which Dick, Samuel, and Daniel
participate in activities symbolic of the New Order: riding bi-
cycles, driving cars; and now Dick is chiefly occupied with
ascents in balloons.) Constance has a present for Dick, too,
which symbolizes her wish to claim him as a son: the watch
she inherited from her father, John Baines, a legendary de-
fender of the Old Order. "'That was father's, ' said Constance.
'He always used to swear by it. When it didn't agree with the
Town Hall, he used to say: 'Then th' Town Hall's wrong.' And
it's curious, the Town Hall *was* wrong.'"

It is significant that, though Constance had offered the watch
to her husband and to her son Cyril, neither would take this
watch of superb accuracy: "My husband would never wear it.
He preferred his own. He had little fancies like that. And Cyril
takes after his father. " Constance wants to give Dick Povey
the watch which Samuel and Cyril would never accept, but only "that is, if he behaves himself. Is he still on with this bal-
looning?" And the irony is that not only does Dick not want the
watch, not only will he not behave himself and give up the bal-

looning--he is about to ascend in a balloon bearing the banner
of the federation which Constance is to sacrifice her life pre-
venting. In marrying Dick, then, Lily Holl proves herself the
true disciple of Constance, marrying again the man Constance
married in Samuel.

This deliberate parallel between the early books and Book IV
is underlined by Constance's musings as she lies dying; after
regretting that Cyril has not come home to be with her, she
reflects:

> Lily and Dick were a treasure to her. In those two
> she really had been lucky. . . they would have been
> startled to know that Constance lovingly looked down
> on both of them. She had unbounded admiration for
> both their hearts; but she thought Dick a little too
> brusque, a little too clownish, to be quite a gentle-
> man. And though Lily was perfectly ladylike, in
> Constance's opinion she lacked backbone, or grit,
> or independence of spirit. Further, Constance con-
> sidered that the disparity of age between them was
> excessive.

In every particular, including the disparity of age, these parallel her own mother's objections to the marriage to Samuel.

This is in part what makes ironic Constance's triumph in
catching her death while casting a vote against federation: at
the same time that she totters out to strike her blow for the
Old Order, her husband Samuel's successor sails over Bursley in a balloon bearing the legend "Vote for Federation!"
Constance triumphs, though, for while Dick's balloon tum-
bles into a field and he breaks his leg, "the mere blind, deaf,
inert forces of reaction" of which Constance is not the least
important member, carry the vote against federation by a large
majority. It is implied, from Mr. Critchlow's evil cackle on
the last page of *The Old Wives' Tale*, that the battle for federation is to go on after all; but it is implied also that the battle
between Lily and Dick will go on just as Constance would have
wished it to.

The whole of Constance's life has been a process of revealing to her "what life is," and the whole of *The Old Wives' Tale*

a maneuvering to create the impact made explicit in the end:

> Constance never pitied herself. She did not consider
> that Fate had treated her very badly. She was not
> very discontented with herself. The invincible com-
> monsense of a sound nature prevented her, in her
> best moments, from feebly dissolving in self-pity.
> She had lived in honesty and kindliness for a fair
> number of years, and she had tasted triumphant
> hours. She was justly respected, she had a position,
> she had dignity, she was well-off. She possessed,
> after all, a certain amount of quiet self-conceit.
> There existed nobody to whom she would "knuckle
> down," or could be asked to "knuckle down." True,
> she was old! So were thousands of other people in
> Bursley. She was in pain. So were thousands of
> other people. With whom would she be willing to ex-
> change lots? She had many dissatisfactions. . . .
> But she rose superior to them. When she surveyed
> her life, and life in general, she would think, with a
> sort of tart but not sour cheerfulness: *"Well, that
> is what life is!"*

V

If middle-class vigor were *The Old Wives' Tale*'s single
quality, the book would be only a serious version of *Denry the
Audacious*. George Orwell, characterizing Dickens, has excel-
lently described the limitations of the urban-bourgeois mind:

> Mentally [Dickens] belongs to the small urban bour-
> geoisie, and he happens to be an exceptionally fine
> specimen of this class, with all the "points," as it
> were, very highly developed. This is partly what
> makes him so interesting. If one wants a modern
> equivalent, the nearest would be H. G. Wells, who
> has had a rather similar history and who obviously
> owes something to Dickens as a novelist. Arnold
> Bennett was essentially the same type, but, unlike
> the other two, he was a midlander, with an indus-

trial and Nonconformist rather than commercial and
Anglican background.
   The great disadvantage, and advantage of the small
urban bourgeois is his limited outlook. He sees the
world as a middle-class world, and everything outside these limits is either laughable or slightly
wicked. On the one hand, he has no contact with in-
dustry or the soil; on the other, no contact with the
governing classes. *

Orwell's classification, which includes Bennett only inci-
dentally, is a good description of the Baines sisters' outlook,
but it does not explain Bennett's own ambiguous position toward his old wives. (Significantly, though, Bennett's was a
commercial rather than an industrial background; he saw the
pottery works as an outsider, had to "get them up" for *Clayhanger*; but he lived in the draper's shop in *The Old Wives'
Tale* as a child.) The ambiguity of Bennett's position is caused
by his being, unlike Dickens, of the exiles: he followed George
Moore and preceded Joyce to France; he wrote all his important work at Fontainebleau; and failure to recognize the peculiar relationships between Fontainebleau and Burslem in
Bennett's work is a failure to understand its nature and quality.
For *The Old Wives' Tale* is an exile's view of Burslem, in a
way an exile's return. The point of view depends upon a complex set of manners and interests which France represented to
the young English writer in 1908.
   What, more precisely, did France mean to Bennett's generation? Something, certainly, connected with the fact that for
twenty years or more it had been producing the most significant
literature in Western Europe--the literature that was the main
determinant of Bennett's techniques. But France meant to Bennett, as to Lambert Strether, a complex of manners and living against which Burslem could be tested.
   The *Journals* and *Paris Nights*, a book written for money,
suggest some of the significance of France for Bennett. It in-

---

*George Orwell, Dickens, Dali and Others: Studies in Pop-
ular Culture* (New York: Reynal and Hitchcock, 1946), p. 24.

volves the apparently permanent myth of the British and Amer-
icans: Paris is a place where exciting experiences can be come
by more readily and cheaply than at home. We in the western
part of the United States fasten this myth on San Francisco,
which cherishes it, and the revelations of our Seattle expatri-
ates roughly parallel Bennett's about Paris, though *Paris
Nights* is less exciting than its title promises. Superior res-
taurants, superior theater (with actresses), articulate literary
coteries, more fashionable clothes, bohemians disdaining fashionable clothes, artistic areas of the city clearly marked off,
historic landmarks surrounding available quarters, prostitutes
with the social elegances and a public following among the fashionable, a foreign colony (British, for Bennett) proud in knowing the ways of the free city. Paris represents away-from-
home, away from parental and parochial restrictions. Bennett
does not credit Paris with new pleasures and sins, but with a
sense of style in exhibiting them. Paris is a theater, devoted
to the dramatic and personal, hostile to the familiar and
utilitarian.

But Paris is also away-from-the-dull-job. There people
do interesting and exciting work. Though the potteries of the
Midlands produce utilitarian objects, they also produce quasi-
artistic work. But the factories *look* functional and the community values follow this appearance. Bennett's Paris is not
only a refuge from the stern father, but also from stern mo-
notony. (When T. S. Eliot came to visit Bennett in Paris, Bennett superciliously asked how Eliot liked working in the bank.
Eliot said bravely that he did not mind it too much.)

By these criteria Sophia fails as a Parisian because she cannot respond properly to excitement. In eloping with Gerald,
she misjudges her real conservatism about experience, her
hatred for the upsets which go along with excitement. Bennett
says nothing overt about sex. But he clearly identifies it with
the sadistic French taste for public guillotinings. The crisis
of Sophia's honeymoon comes in her reluctant trip to view the
execution and in her inability--and finally, Gerald's--to participate in the general feeling. When the "marriage" fails, she
becomes ill of the mysterious emotional fever inherited from
nineteenth-century novels, and, on recovering, rejects the
presumably most exciting and flexible of occupations, being a

courtesan. She responds to the threat of conscience by return-
ing to her training in business and presently becomes a professional mother to tourists.

Sophia rejects intense experience because she loves orderliness and does not have the stomach for the strange, the exciting, the eternally flexible. When she has a chance for le-
gitimate romance, with Chirac, a dilettantism of the exciting
is again the barrier. Chirac is the slightly eccentric hero of
interesting work. He reports whatever will keep the public
awake over its morning paper. But he wants to participate in
the making of headlines, and his long-shot venture from Paris
in the balloon--filled with hot air--symbolizes his separation
from Sophia, who feels comfortable in cool air. (Constance,
significantly, has her feud with a balloon--Dick Povey's.)
The tension in Book II comes from the reader's urging Sophia
to take chances in the name of experience while she continually chooses security. Bennett's reservation about her--and
the basis of his understanding--is that, always connecting the
exciting and the traumatic, she withdraws from all but economic participation in life.

Sophia, rather than Henry Earlforward of *Riceyman Steps*,
is Bennett's greatest miser. She hoards both money and affection. Apparently a dramatic personality, she is blind to the
color and detail of the dramatic view of life. The appearance
of Peel-Swynnerton at the pension brings on her second illness, this time shock at recognizing the vacuum of affection
that she has created.

Her return to Bursley is in part a return to judgment on her
life. She partly recovers the capacity for affection, but she
does not pass the test of having *seen* the world. She fails to
impress herself upon the knowledgeable as a woman of the
world. Her clothes, her dog, and her manner are chic. She
is not inexperienced and she has had her dark night of the soul.
She is far from ignorant of day-to-day French life; in fact, her
confidence comes from having excelled in it. But instead of
seeing France through the most sympathetic and intelligent
foreign eyes, she has seen a generation of British tourists;
and it is only at the Rutland Hotel that Sophia realizes she has
mistaken the respectable efficiency of the Pension Frensham

for true elegance. She has not seen the *dramatic representation* of French life which Bennett takes for its essence.

The novel is thus built upon two main themes: the Old Order's vitality triumphing over everything but the physiological process itself; and Bennett's ambiguous attitude toward the manners and interests comprising French culture of the period and the relative crudeness of the aristocrat of the north. The structure of the novel derives from this ambiguity. Constance is the blind force of reaction, the rare and fortunate person for whom the mold is an exact fit. The conception of the novel began with Constance; Sophia had to be added because of the ambiguousness of Bennett's convictions, of which she is in part the agent--"provincial" is her epithet for Constance in the end--and in part the unconscious illustration. Sophia represents the other side of the midland temperament--and of life-- but she had to be taken to France and then brought back to Bursley to enforce the ambiguity behind Bennett's concept of the primitive.

Sophia's first mediation--mostly unconscious on her part-- comes in her reactions to the complex scene of France, for in this novel Bennett avoids the crudity of a commentator as in "The Death of Simon Fuge, " and creates an unconscious commentator in Sophia. Gerald Scales and the trader who brings Joseph to Egypt in Mann's novel have the same structural purpose: they bring the representative of a more primitive culture to emotions and tastes alike subject to a complication and rarefication not found in the original culture.

Orwell says rightly that every novelist has a "message." Bennett's message lies in a mediation between the primitive conceived as the commercial aristocrat, and the aspiration to a more complex set of morals and manners. For *The Old Wives' Tale* it can be at least partly summarized: those people back in that commercial-industrial town had a very low standing in the scale of Parisian values, but their lives were formidable, not tragic, because they had the vitality of an unquestioned tradition.

## 6. *Clayhanger*

PERHAPS most directly of Bennett's novels, *Clayhanger* mediates between taste and primitivism. There is force in the rise of the primitive hero, Darius Clayhanger. His destitute childhood, his rescue by old Mr. Shushions, his climb to power could, with differences, have been told by Dreiser or Farrell. But *Clayhanger* is something more than a naturalistic novel of this sort. Its theme (which on the surface seems two themes, the clash between father and son, and the love of Edwin for Hilda) is in reality the contest between power and taste--the contest between Edwin's real father, Darius the printer, and his ideal father, Osmond Orgreave, for him.

### I

What the book has to say is that Edwin is not his father. He never becomes a father on any terms. Edwin is a son, like Hans Castorp and Paul Morel, but one described by a writer not particularly sympathetic to sons. Bennett deified the *will* too strongly to present with entire success an Edwin in the role of Hero. Edwin's is the story of the potential artist, the potential man of taste, struggling toward the light of culture. It is the story of a family fortune--of the man who made it, and of the man who inherited and conserved it; of two ways of life--that of the rise to power, and that of the search for taste. For all the reservations, Edwin comes closest to embodying Bennett's major conflict.

## II

It is also, of course, the story of the love between Edwin and Hilda. But Hilda is in reality only a sort of mediator between Darius and Osmond. Janet Orgreave is the girl Edwin would have married had Osmond won the main moral conflict. "Janet had every quality that he could desire, that he could even think of. " But after his father crushes his intention to become an architect, Edwin's soul is lamed, and he cannot enter fully into the Orgreave world. He feels that the Orgreaves are too fine for him. Toward Charlie Orgreave, his old school chum, he feels the "half-sneering awe of a provincial. " Hilda is a compromise. She is not so stylish as Janet Orgreave, but she too has a measure of culture. She is a compromise between the Clayhangers and Orgreaves:

> She was no more worldly than Maggie and Clara
> were worldly. Than they, she had no more skill
> to be sociable. And in appearance she was scarce-
> ly more stylish. But she was not as they, and it was
> useless vindictively to disparage her by pretend-
> ing that she was. She could be passionate concern-
> ing Victor Hugo. She was capable of disturbing her-
> self about the abstract question of belief.

The most important thing about Hilda, however, is that she is a creature of the Orgreaves, almost their creation. Edwin could have thought her ugly, at first, if the Orgreaves had not told him she was beautiful. He does not love Hilda so much as he loves the Orgreaves' conception of her: "The consoling thing was that the Orgreaves had always expressed high esteem for Hilda. He leaned on the Orgreaves. "

There is a less important, though significant, side to Edwin's choice of Hilda. She is a mannish woman. Edwin is described frequently as an old maid, and he does seem to have some of the characteristics which distinguish Marcel, Hans Castorp, and Paul Morel from the stronger brothers and fathers in three novels of taste. Marcel has Albertine; Hans has Clavdia Chauchat, who resembles the boy he loved in his adolescence; and Paul Morel prefers the aggressive Clara to gen-

tle Miriam. Edwin likes Hilda for her voice, which is re-
markably deep, her hair, which is "not like a girl's hair, "
her conversation, "utterly unlike girls' conversation, " and her
trick of straightening her shoulders. He thought her "less feminine than masculine."But that does not necessarily explain why
Bennett should have chosen to marry Edwin to Hilda rather
than to a daughter of Osmond's. Supposing Janet to have been
too feminine, Bennett as author could have created another,
more masculine, Orgreave girl for Edwin. The earlier explanation of Edwin's choice is more significant for the novel.

### III

The three books of *Clayhanger* are titled, "His Vocation, "
"His Love, " and "His Freedom. " They could with justifica-
tion be titled, "Edwin and Darius Clayhanger, " "Edwin and
Osmond Orgreave, " and "The Compromise"--three titles which
suggest the whole story of *Clayhanger*. The first book begins
with Edwin's childhood, interrupts for a long résumé of Da-
ius' childhood, and recommences Edwin's story with his growing resolve to be an architect. This book culminates in Darius' crushing Edwin's resolution and temporarily defeating
the influence of Osmond Orgreave, who had been the driving
force behind Edwin's determination to become an architect.

The opening sentence of the second book stresses the fact
that seven years have passed. During these seven years Darius
Clayhanger has had complete domination over Edwin. But now,
with the new book, the architect Orgreave again asserts him-
self--not to direct Edwin's vocation this time, but to put together what is left of his life after his vocation has been ruined.
He encourages Edwin in building a more splendid new house,
the cultivation of manners, reading books, playing music, and
finally, in selecting a wife who is superior to the Five Towns.
The second book could end with the marriage of Hilda and Edwin, if it were not for one thing: Edwin's father is still the
real victor. At the end of Book I, he has triumphed over Osmond Orgreave in the matter of Edwin's vocation, the triumph
of industrialism, of the printing business, over architecture,
or taste. Now he triumphs again. It is clear that Darius has
already made his son's marriage to Hilda impossible, before

her sudden mysterious elopement with George Cannon makes it openly so. Edwin, cut off from marriage by his father's refusal of a subsistence wage, would have been forced to wait until Darius' death.

Edwin recognizes his father's second victory at the closing of the scene in which Darius refuses:

> Miserable, despicable baseness. Did the old devil suppose that he would be capable of asking his wife to find the resources which he himself could not bring? . . .
>
> As he stood furious and impotent in the hall, he thought, with his imagination quickened by the memory of Mr. Shushions: "When you're old, and I've *got* you--" he clenched his fists and his teeth--"When I've got you and you can't help yourself, by God it'll be my turn!"
>
> And he meant it.

This is the real end of Book II--the second defeat of the architect by the printer. The next and last scene, with its discovery that Hilda has inexplicably eloped, does nothing but gloss over the fact that for Edwin Hilda has already been lost, and with her, temporarily at least, his hopes for a life of culture and of taste as an equal member of the Orgreave clan.

Book III, which Bennett called "His Freedom, " records the final defeat of Darius Clayhanger and the triumph of the architect. But again the architect triumphs by default. Darius is not the man to yield to any human opponent. Like Sophia and Constance and all of Bennett's strong heroes, he bows only to disease and death. And yet Darius' disease is a peculiar triumph for the architect son whose will he crushed, for it is softening of the brain. Bennett makes much of the fact that softening of the brain destroys the will; his most impressive irony is that Edwin, who has no will of his own, should be given complete domination over his father, even to the point of deciding whether the old man shall grow a beard. (And even in this small matter, Edwin, characteristically, hesitates.)

Some of the impressiveness that informs *Clayhanger* comes from such a father being dressed and fed by such a son. There

is something lacking in the love story of Edwin and Hilda which
is not lacking in the story of Hilda and George Cannon. Edwin
is not the one man for Hilda, and *Clayhanger* suffers in proportion as their love story takes the center stage. But Edwin
is the one man for Darius--the one who could make his loss
of will most ironic, his death most tragic; and it is that which
makes the disease and death scenes of *Clayhanger* so memorable. Had Edwin been a natural bully, rather than a Hamlet
of the Five Towns, the spectacle of his triumph would be merely disgusting.

While Edwin's father over a period of years is dying of softening of the brain, Osmond Orgreave begins for a third time
to assert his influence. But the old printer until his death
stands athwart the influence of the architect. Even his sickness
becomes the obstacle that prevents Orgreave from taking Edwin to London. The chapter which describes this third defeat
for Osmond Orgreave, "A Change of Mind," presents the problem straightforwardly as a choice between architect and father.
(London, while inferior to Paris in the Bennett hierarchy, is
often a substitute symbol.)

> . . . [Orgreave] had urgently invited Edwin to ac-
> company them. At first Edwin had instinctively re-
> plied that it was impossible. He could not leave
> home. He had never been to London: a journey to
> London presented itself to him as an immense en-
> terprise, almost a piece of culpable self-indul-
> gence (this from a man of thirty). And then, under
> the stimulus of Osmond's energetic and adventur-
> ous temperament, he said to himself: "Why not?
> Why shouldn't I?"
>
> The arguments favoured his going. It was absurd
> and scandalous that he had never been to London:
> he ought for his self-respect to depart thither at
> once. . . .

So it is settled that Edwin will go to London, and once more
the architect seems about to triumph. But on the day Edwin
is to go, a crisis in Darius' disease occurs: he is no longer

able to distinguish between his knife and fork. This small relapse changes Edwin's mind; he will not go to London:

> In his bedroom, after tea, Edwin fought against
> the gloomy influence, but uselessly. The inherent
> and appalling sadness of existence enveloped and
> chilled him. He gazed at the row of his books. He
> had done no regular reading of late. Why read? He
> gazed at the screen in front of his bed, covered with
> neat memoranda. How futile! Why go to London? He
> would only have to come back from London! And
> then he said resistingly: "I *will* go to London." But
> as he said it, aloud, he knew well that he would not
> go.

Bennett understands this scene to be crucial, and after Darius' death, Bennett comments on Edwin's new freedom:
"He bought books surpassing those books of Tom Orgreave
which had once seemed so hopelessly beyond his reach. He
went to the theatre. He went to concerts. He took holidays. He
had been to London, *and more than once.*"
At last the architect triumphs, but only by default. The
founding father is still the real victor. In *The Magic Mountain*,
Naptha and Settembrini contend for the soul of Hans, the en-
gineer-architect. After their battle is resolved, the book loses
some of its impetus, and after the battle of *Clayhanger* is resolved by Darius' death, the story never recovers its drive.
Hilda's return provides a compromise, but does not entirely
gloss over the fact that for Edwin the final catastrophe was not
her going, but the defeat of his ambitions. Early in the book
that first catastrophe occurs, and Bennett later comments:

> He has forgiven his father for having thwarted his
> supreme ambition; long ago he had forgiven his fa-
> ther; though, curiously, he had never quite forgiv-
> en Mrs. Hamps for her share in the catastrophe. He
> honestly thought he had recovered from the catas-
> trophe undisfigured, even unmarked. He knew not
> that he would never be the same man again, and that

his lightest gesture, and his lightest glance were
touched with the wistfulness of resignation.

A wistful hero is touching, but he can be wearying when his
career is sustained through a trilogy. Edwin's tragedy was
that his father killed his ambition. Darius' tragedy was that
he died. But Bennett's tragedy was that he killed off Darius so
early in the trilogy. Osmond Orgreave needs someone to fight.

## IV

The picture of Darius' rise, struggle for his son, and disease and death is so forceful that it is possible to miss the
importance of the Orgreaves as culture symbols. But without
them the book would be a meaningless chronology of incidents,
culminating in the death of Darius, two-thirds through the
book, and padded out to its conclusion by a partly irrelevant
account of Edwin's maturity and final winning of Hilda Lessways. Fortunately, *Clayhanger* is something more than that.

An analysis of the novel, then, must be made in terms of the
two major antagonists. Bennett himself accords this conflict
an importance which makes him place at strategic intervals the
scenes in which the Orgreaves take part. Edwin's spiritual
sonship to Osmond Orgreave is necessary to make meaningful
his relation with his actual father.

Bennett loses no time in introducing the theme of the Orgreaves. On page three of *Clayhanger,* Charlie Orgreave,
nicknamed "The Sunday, " is introduced. He is Edwin's best
friend, and crucial to the whole book, because through him Edwin meets the substitute father; Charlie is the *deus ex machina*
of Edwin's introduction into the Orgreave clan. The note of the
Orgreave boy's superior taste is sounded on page four:

> "Rats!" said the Sunday with finality. In the pro-
> nunciation of this word the difference between his
> accent and Edwin's came out clear. The Sunday's
> accent was less local; there was a hint of a short "e"
> sound in the "a", and a briskness about the conso-
> nants, that Edwin could never have compassed. The
> Sunday's accent was as carelessly superior as his

clothes. Evidently the Sunday had someone at home
who had not learnt the art of speech in the Five
Towns.

The "someone at home" is the Orgreave father, and his influence is not long in making itself felt. Osmond crystallizes
Edwin's determination to become an architect. This incident
begins casually, with Edwin inquiring after his friend Charlie,
who is now away at school, significantly, in France.

> Less than a year ago Charlie Orgreave had been "the
> Sunday," had been "old Perish-in-the-attempt," and
> now he was a student in Besançon University, unap-
> proachable, extraordinarily romantic; and he, Ed-
> win, remained in his father's shop! He had been
> aware that Charlie had gone to Besançon University,
> but he had not realised it effectively till this mo-
> ment. The realisation blew discontent into a flame,
> which fed on the further perception that evidently the
> Orgreave family were a gay, jolly crowd of cronies
> together; not in the least like parents and children;
> their home life must be something fundamentally
> different from his.

The stage is set for Edwin's infatuation with Orgreave as a
father image; his determination to become an architect now
needs only the smallest impetus to become the wish of a life-
time. Orgreave admires the window of the Sytch Pottery, and
Edwin thinks that he "had never heard the word 'beautiful' ut-
tered in quite that tone, except by women. . . . But Mr. Orgreave was not a woman; he was a man of the world, he was
almost *the* man of the world; and the subject of his adjective
was a window!"
This is a revelation for Edwin, and it is followed by another,
when Orgreave shows him that the Sytch Pottery itself has
"exquisite pointing." This revelation is all Edwin needs:

> He would never have thought so but for the accident
> of the walk with Mr. Orgreave; he might have spent
> his whole life in the town, and never troubled him-

self a moment about the Sytch Pottery. Nevertheless he now, by an act of sheer faith, suddenly, miraculously and genuinely regarded it as an exquisitely beautiful edifice, on a plane with the edifices of the capitals of Europe, and as a feast for discerning eyes. "I like architecture very much," he added. And this too was said with such feverish conviction that Mr. Orgreave was quite moved.

The next day Edwin takes a walk again past the Sytch Pottery, and, standing in front of it, vows that he will write his father the letter announcing his decision to be an architect. It is characteristic of the son that the decision cannot be announced to Darius' face. Osmond Orgreave has captured the spiritual Edwin, but Darius' hold on the physical one is foreordained by Edwin's timidity. The letter proves to be disastrous, and Book I ends with the defeat of Edwin and Mr. Orgreave. Edwin will remain in the printing shop.

V

There is no need to multiply the examples of Edwin's slavery to the Orgreave code. He is somewhat in the position of the hero of *Brideshead Revisited*; each member of the Orgreave family represents for him some special virtue of taste, or of manners. There is spectacled Tom Orgreave, who shows him that books are treasures: "He saw that a book might be more than reading matter, might be a bibelot, a curious jewel, to satisfy the lust of the eye and of the hand." It is typical of the Orgreaves' strategic spot in *Clayhanger,* that this one revelation of the value of books should precipitate one of Edwin's most important quarrels with his own father--a quarrel that occupies three chapters, "Money," "The Insult," and "The Sequel."

And then of course there is Charlie Orgreave, his old friend, who introduces him into the Orgreave home for the first time, a visit of which Bennett comments: "It was the first time that there had ever been a question of him visiting a private house, except his aunt's, at night. To him the moment marked an epoch, the inception of freedom."

There is Janet Orgreave, who first makes him aware of manners, of clothes, and of the excitement of rising in the social scale, who makes him think for the first time the recurrent Bennett phrase, "so this is what life is." Janet is his destined wife, at least in his mind and in hers, though there is never an open avowal between them. He feels that she is too fine for him and takes Hilda instead. Janet, as well as Tom, is responsible for an important clash between Edwin and his father. Her innocent request that Edwin order Edwin Arnold's *The Light of Asia* for her precipitates a scene in which Darius, in front of the entire printing staff, reprimands Edwin for taking it on himself to order books through the Clayhanger printing business, since he, Darius, had decided not to handle new books. (The scene is practically a textbook prescription for the realistic symbolizing of a major conflict.) Again, on the day of Hilda's and Edwin's betrothal, a significant conversation occurs: '"It's awfully funny,' he said. 'I scarcely know anything about you, and yet--' 'I'm Janet's friend!' she answered. Perhaps it was the delicatest reproof of his imagined distrust."

Janet remains important as a culture mediator and an instrument for bringing Hilda and Edwin together. After ten years she reunites the couple by bringing Hilda's son George back from Brighton. (Edwin gets acquainted with George through Janet, and his attachment to Hilda's son brings Hilda back to Bursley.)

And last, of course, there is Mrs. Orgreave, who unites in her person and ménage the charms of established culture. She embodies Edwin's ideas of the Orgreave home, which "like its mistress . . . seemed to exhale a silent and calm authority, based on historic tradition."

But most of all Osmond Orgreave is Darius' enemy in the struggle for Edwin. All the Clayhangers recognize this--most of all his sister Clara, the antithesis of the Orgreaves, who takes over as the family protagonist when Darius dies (with her name on his lips). Her symbolical antagonism to everything Orgreave is stressed even in the third book of the trilogy, *These Twain*.

> . . . [Edwin] gave away a great deal of Mr. Orgreave's wisdom without mentioning the origin of

the gift. Thus occasionally Clara would say cutting-
ly: "I know where you've picked that up. You've
picked that up from Mr. Orgreave." The young
man Benbow to whom . . . Clara had been so queer-
ly engaged, also received from Edwin considerable
quantities of Mr. Orgreave. But the fellow was only
a decent, dull, pushing, successful ass, and quite
unable to assimilate Mr. Orgreave; Edwin could
never comprehend how Clara . . . could mate herself to a fellow like Benbow.

Orgreave, with his "aristocratic deportment, his equality to
every situation, and his extraordinary skill in keeping his dignity and his distance during encounters with Darius," is the
man with whom Darius Clayhanger has to battle for possession
of his son. Darius has no intention of yielding the battle to Edwin's other father, though Darius has often wondered how "he,
so common, had begotten a creature so subtly aristocratic . . .
aristocratic was the word." But he intends to keep Edwin. That
he succeeds is the core of *Clayhanger*.

Thanks to Darius, there is a grimness and drama in the
quarrels between father and son that even Sophia's struggle
with Mrs. Baines does not have. In entering sympathetically
into Darius' mind, Bennett uses to advantage a device that he
does not use for Mrs. Baines and Constance--the set symbol.
His "little boy from the Bastille" explains Darius' tyranny and
his tremendous will that Edwin become a printer. Bennett's
method of establishing this symbol is both the strength and the
weakness of *Clayhanger*.

Bennett's dilemma was the necessity of presenting immediately the quality of two lives, not parallel as in *The Old
Wives' Tale*, but separated by a generation. Dividing the book
into sections as he did for Constance and Sophia would have
been difficult, for Darius strongly influences Edwin's actions.
If the reader is to see the conflict as Bennett sees it--a conflict with justice on the side of the culture-seeker, but the idio-
syncrasy of the individual personality and the righteousness
of the father's cause as a still fuller truth--Darius' reasons
must be presented along with Edwin's. Yet a lumped history of
Darius is necessary to the conception of the novel as a whole,

for the high degree of survival of the boy in the man--unper-
ceived by the public, but clearly felt by the man himself--
is one of Bennett's better insights and is developed also in
*Riceyman Steps*. The "boy from the Bastille" is, in Bennett's
interpretation, basic in the tyrant father.

The beginning is not wholly a failure. In spite of inevitable
summarizing, the "Child-Man" chapters contain some of the
most forceful material Bennett wrote in the direct Zola tradition. Even in summary, Darius has force. And even with so
much material to cover, Bennett's capacity for scene is high
enough to give a partially dramatized effect. He symbolizes
months of Darius' experience in four significant days--Da-
rius' first day at work, his second day, his last day, and the
memorable day in the workhouse. The irony is effective, if
broad, and Bennett's own interest in processes communicates
itself in the descriptions of Darius' labors as a mold-runner
and handle-maker.

In spite of failures, Bennett, in *Clayhanger,* succeeds with
two interwoven themes, both of which depend for their force
upon the clash between different generations and different mores: the theme of fathers and sons, and of the stubborn man
of will cut down at the height of his pride and strength. The
basic building block of the first theme is the series of subdued
crises that constituted Bennett's major technical achievement
in the Constance section of *Old Wives' Tale.* Bennett is a master of the minor tension like the opening conflict over Edwin's
future:

> "Eh!" said Mrs. Hamps enthusiastically after a
> trifling pause. "It does me good when I think what
> a *help* you'll be to your father in the business, with
> that clever head of yours!"
> She gazed at him fondly.
> Now this was Edwin's chance. He did not wish to
> be any help at all to his father in the business. He
> had other plans for himself. He had never mentioned
> them before, because his father had never talked to
> him about his future career, apparently assuming
> that he would go into the business. He had been
> waiting for his father to begin. "Surely, " he had

said to himself, "father's bound to speak to me
sometime about what I'm going to do, and when he
does I shall just tell him. " But his father had never
begun; and by timidity, negligence, and perhaps ill-
luck, Edwin had thus arrived at his last day at school
with the supreme question not merely unsolved but
unattacked. Oh! He blamed himself--any ordinary
boy (he thought) would have discussed such a question naturally long ago. After all it was not a crime,
it was no cause for shame, to wish not to be a printer. Yet he was ashamed! Absurd! He blamed himself. But he also blamed his father. Now, however,
in responding to his aunt's remark, he could remedy
all the past by simply and boldly stating that he did
not want to follow his father. It would be unpleasant,
of course, but the worst shock would be over in a
moment, like the drawing of a tooth. He had merely
to utter certain words. He must utter them. They
were perfectly easy to say, and they were also of
the greatest urgency. "I don't want to be a printer. " He mumbled them over in his mind. "I don't
want to be a printer. . . . " What could it matter to
his father whether he was a printer or not? Seconds,
minutes, seemed to pass. He knew that if he was
so inconceivably craven as to remain silent, his
self-respect would never recover from the blow.
Then, in response to Mrs. Hamps's prediction about
his usefulness to his father in the business, he said,
with a false-jaunty, unconvinced, unconvincing air:
    "Well, that remains to be seen. "
    This was all that he could accomplish. It seemed
as if he had looked death in the face, and drawn away.
    "Remains to be seen!" Auntie Clara repeated,
with a hint of startled pain, due to this levity.
    He was mute. No one suspected as he sat there,
so boyish, so wistful, and uneasily squirming, that
he was agonised to the very center of his being. All
the time, in his sweating soul, he kept trying to per-
suade himself: "I've given them a hint, anyhow! I've
given them a hint, anyhow!"

> Mr. Clayhanger, completely ignoring Edwin's re-
> ply to his aunt and her somewhat shocked repetition
> of it, turned towards his son suddenly and said, in
> a manner friendly but serious, a manner that as-
> sumed everything, a manner that begged the ques-
> tion, unconscious even that there was a question:
> "I shall be out the better part o' tomorrow. I want
> ye to be sure to be in the shop all afternoon. . . ."

Technically this scene is the opposite of the long, evenly developed scene at the beginning of *The Man of Property*. Galsworthy's method of presenting the typical is to make sure, like
a good hostess, that we have met and chatted with everybody.
Bennett's is to produce a scene short, low-keyed, but with
mounting tension. Constance in her parents' bed for the first
time as a married woman recoils from the "chasm" opened by
a quarrel over paper collars. So Edwin, in an excess of relief
over his father's gruff friendliness about the first "bit o' business, " gets courage to say he wants to be an architect--and
the tension passes when Darius, who "attached no importance
of any kind to this avowal of a preference, " again ignores the
issue. In *Clayhanger* as in *The Old Wives' Tale,* these page-
or-two crises are the essential method of enlivening the typical.

Through small crisis after small crisis, the book builds an
impressive clash between two generations and two ways of life.
Darius' fury at each crisis furnishes the energy, and under-
lying all his reactions to Edwin is the escape from the workhouse, the "little boy from the Bastille. " Darius' pleasure
in Edwin's handling of his first business assignment comes
from the view that Edwin has "lived in cotton wool, " and his
overwhelming gratitude at the saving of the floor is caused by
this same underestimation of Edwin's potential strength. Further irony is given to Edwin's heroism by the fact that it dooms
him to the life of a printer from which he might otherwise have
escaped. It is in gratitude for his saving the shop that Darius
begins to delegate to his son the authorities that gradually en-
mesh him in the printing business and make escape infeasible.
Edwin's quick and cool action in this crisis is in keeping with
his character. He is a Hamlet without an Elsinore--a boy in-

capable of facing in cold blood the task of freeing himself from
his father, but perfectly capable of action if a situation is
thrust upon him.

In the crucial quarrel over architecture, it is the "boy from
the Bastille" who rises to crush Edwin:

> As with gathering passion the eyes of Darius assault-
> ed the window pane, Darius had a painful intense
> vision of that miracle, his own career. Edwin's
> grand misfortune was that he was blind to the mir-
> acle. Edwin had never seen the little boy in the
> Bastille. But Darius saw him always, the infant who
> had begun life at a rope's-end. Every hour of Darius'
> present existence was really an astounding marvel to
> Darius. He could not read the newspaper without
> thinking how wonderful it was that he should be able
> to read. . . . It was wonderful that he was not living
> in a two-roomed cottage. He never came into his
> house by the side-entrance without feeling proud that
> the door gave on to a preliminary passage and not
> direct into the living room. . . . It was wonderful
> that he had a piano, and that his girls could play it
> and sing. It was wonderful that he had paid twenty-
> eight shillings a term for his son's education, in
> addition to book-money. Twenty-eight shillings a
> term! And once, a penny a week was considered
> enough and twopence generous! Through sheer splen-
> did wilful pride he had kept his son at school till the
> lad was sixteen, going on seventeen! Seventeen, not
> seven! He had had the sort of pride in his son that a
> man may have in an idle, elegant, and absurdly ex-
> pensive woman. . . . He often took keen pleasure
> in speculating upon the demeanour of his father, his
> mother, his little sister, could they have seen him
> in his purple and his grandeur. They were all dead.
> And those days were fading, fading, gone, with their
> unutterable, intolerable shame and sadness, intol-
> erable even in memory.

The same conception heightens the pathos of Darius' illness and death:

> A nurse herself sped them from the room, in her quality of mistress of the room. And when she and Maggie and Darius were alone together she went to the bedside and spoke softly to her patient. She was so neat and bright and white and striped, and so perfect in every detail, that she might have been a model taken straight from a shop-window. Her figure illuminated the dusk. An incredible luxury for the little boy from the Bastille! But she was one of the many wonderful things he had earned.

Bennett's subsidiary device for imparting depth to the personal struggle between Edwin and Darius--a struggle begun in the clash over Edwin's career, but continued in day-by-day irritations which only hint at the fundamental disagreement between them--is not to immerse it in time, but in significant social and political events. Bennett's liberalism is less important here than his use of politics to dramatize the solidifying bitterness between father and son. The most significant thing about this technique, though, is that the political clashes between Edwin and Darius seldom appear as set scenes, and never as prolonged and intensive scenes; Bennett reserves for the father and son clashes over Edwin's choice of a career, friends, or amusements the fully treated quarrels which give body to *Clayhanger*.

Bennett's manner of using political and social change is illustrated by the chapter "Father and Son after Seven Years," which begins with a 1910 equivalent of Dos Passos' newsreel to set the social background:

> Board schools had been opened in Bursley, wondrous affairs, with ventilation. . . . A Jew had been made Master of the Rolls: spectacle at which England shivered, and then, perceiving no sign of disaster, shrugged its shoulders. Irish members had taught the House of Commons how to talk for twenty-four hours without a pause. The wages of the

agricultural labourer had sprung into the air and
leaped over the twelve shilling bar into regions of
opulence. Moody and Sankey had found and conquered
England for Christ. Landseer and Livingstone had
died, and the provinces could not decide whether
"Dignity and Impudence" or the penetration of Africa
was the more interesting feat. Herbert Spencer had
published his "Study of Sociology, " Matthew Arnold
his "Literature and Dogma" and Frederick Farrar
his Life of his Lord; but here the provinces had no
difficulty in deciding, for they had only heard of the
last. Every effort had been made to explain by per-
suasion and by force to the working-man that trade-
unions were inimical to his true welfare, and none
had succeeded, so stupid was he. The British Army
had been employed to put reason into the noddle of
a town called Northampton which was furious because an atheist had not been elected to Parliament.
Pullman cars, "The Pirates of Penzance, " Henry
Irving's Hamlet, spellingbees, and Captain Webb's
channel swim had all proved that there were novel-
ties under the sun. . . . Ireland had all but died of
hunger, but had happily been saved to enjoy the ben-
efits of Coercion. The Young Men's Christian Association had been born again in the splendour of
Exeter Hall. Bursley itself had entered on a new
career as a chartered borough, with Mayor, alder-
men, and councillors all in chains of silver.

But "to Edwin, Darius was exactly the same father, and for
Darius Edwin was still aged sixteen. . . . They both of them
went on living in the assumption that the world had stood still
in those seven years between 1873 and 1880." Nevertheless,
the political declension that is to symbolize Darius' growing
world-weariness and bad temper has begun:

Darius was possibly a little uneasy in his mind
about the world. Possibly there had just now begun
to form in his mind the conviction, in which most
men die, that all was not quite well with the world,

and that in particular his native country had con-
tracted a fatal malady since he was a boy.

He was a printer, and yet the general election had
not put sunshine into his heart.

Three pages later Darius rages at Edwin for joining the Liberal Club, although Darius has been a member for many years.
The daily cleavage, which breaks into argument only sporadi-
cally, comes out in a scene between Edwin and Hilda:

"You aren't ashamed of your own opinions, are
you?" she demanded, with a hint in her voice that
she was ready to be scornful.

"You 'know all the time' I'm not, " he repeated.
. . . "Don't you?" he added curtly.

She remained silent.

"Don't you?" he said more loudly. And as she
offered no reply, he went on, marvelling at what was
coming out of his mouth. "I'll tell you what I'm
ashamed of. I'm ashamed of seeing my father lose
his temper. Now you know!"

Darius collapses clutching a copy of the *Signal* carrying the
announcement that has just brought Edwin his highest political ecstasy--the announcement of Gladstone's Home Rule Bill.
Darius' first acts after the collapse are to resign from the
Liberal Club and join the Conservative. And when Darius dies,
the boisterous crowd celebrating the Tory victory brings Edwin his first realization of freedom:

It was in his resentment, in the hard setting of
his teeth as he confirmed himself in the rightness
of his own opinions, that he first began to realise
an individual freedom. "I don't care if we're beaten
forty times, " his thoughts ran, "I'll be a more out-
and-out Radical than ever! I don't care, and I don't
care!" And he felt sturdily that he was free. The
chain was at last broken that had bound together
those two beings so dissimilar, antagonistic, and
ill-matched,--Edwin Clayhanger and his father.

   While Darius lives, Bennett works to indicate distinct stages
of Edwin's development, to set these against a background of
social change, and to symbolize the cleavage between father
and son in terms of the Liberal-Conservative struggle. As
long as the conflict between Darius and the Edwin-Orgreave
clique continues, Bennett is explicit about dates and events.
The beginnings of the first three parts unmistakably demarcate
stages:

   It was a breezy Friday in July, 1872. . . .

   Seven years passed. Towards the end of April,
   1880, on a Saturday morning. . . .

   Four and a half years later, on a Tuesday night in
   April, 1886, Edwin. . . .

But once Darius' death has resolved the issue, Bennett returns
to his *Old Wives' Tale* subtlety in handling time and, at the
beginning of Part IV, uses the technique for an *Old Wives' Tale*
purpose--to suggest the years between Darius' death and the
rediscovery of Hilda as years without too much meaning, made
up of small events and quarrels. Part IV begins in the familiar
way: "It was Auntie Hamps' birthday. 'She must be quite fifty-
nine,' said Maggie. 'Oh! Stuff!' Edwin contradicted her curtly.
'She can't be anything like as much as that.'"
   The best section of *Clayhanger* examines Darius' illness and
death. Its intensity surpasses any passage of similar length in
*The Old Wives' Tale,* and it remains clear in the memory after
many of the carefully documented scenes in the earlier book
have faded. In Bennett the impressiveness of death as a phenomenon is greatest when the character who is cut down by
death is a man of extremely strong will. It is the founder of
the line for whom there is cause for mourning. Bennett shares
with few but Mann a sincere appreciation of the virtues of the
builder. It is for the Dariuses of his books that Bennett reserves the carefully drawn death scenes, not the Edwins. There
is real power in the spectacle of a man of Darius' intense will
dying from as degrading a disease as softening of the brain.
The death scenes are all the more impressive because they

filter to us through the consciousness of Edwin, who has the
Proustian appreciation of a dilettante to make more subtle the
nuances of the phenomenon:

> . . . he was preoccupied with the thought of the ma-
> lignant and subtle power working secretly in his fa-
> ther's brain. How could the doctor tell? What was
> the process of softening: Did his father know, in
> that sick brain of his, that he was condemned; or
> did he hope to recover? Now, as he leaned against
> the mantelpiece, protruding his body in an easy pos-
> ture, he might have been any ordinary man, and
> not a victim; he might have been a man of business
> relaxing after a long day of hard and successful cer-
> ebral activity. . . .

Edwin's Proustian ability to be a talented spectator is indi-
cated several times before the death scenes occur, notably in
a scene in which he perceives that hidden in the bulky case of
his sister Clara's pregnant body is still the willful child Clara.
"The impartial and unmoved spectator that sat somewhere in
Edwin, as in everybody who possesses artistic sensibility,
watching his secret life as from a conning tower, thought how
strange this was."

But Edwin reaches his supreme emotional insight at the
spectacle of death: "No! He would not fetch Maggie and he
would not go for the doctor. What use? . . . In the solemnity
of the night he was glad that an experience tremendous and
supreme had been vouchsafed to him. He knew now what the
will-to-live was. He saw life naked, stripped of everything in-
essential. He saw life and death together." No one passage can
give the *savoring* of death which is Edwin's contribution to
*Clayhanger*. It does not emerge through the wording--Bennett
was not master of the subtle phrase--but through the reiteration of Edwin's day-by-day spying on the tiniest changes
in Darius' condition. For it is Edwin's greatness, his flair, to
be particularly sensitive spectator at the crises of others. Da-
rius-watching-at-Edwin's-deathbed would fail in a double sense
--there would be nothing impressive about the death of an Edwin, and if there were, Darius would not be artist enough to

perceive it. It is not the financiers, the Christopher Newmans,
the Josephs-in-Egypt of literature who make good deathbed
watchers; but the little Hannos, Hans Castorps, and the Mar-
cels--the second, and the third, generations.

Thus the death of the strong grandmother in *Remembrance
of Things Past* is at once the most poignant and the most subtly treated passage in the novel--a vision of the grandmother
with her proud face surmounted by a crown of writhing leeches.
And we see this scene through the eyes of the same Marcel
who can be so tedious about his own sufferings and degrada-
tions. Another scene which depends for some of its impact on
the nature of the sensitive observer is the funeral of Hans
Castorp's grandfather (the upright old man who had, as he
grew older, to rest his chin on his ruff to keep his head from
trembling). And Auntie Hamps, in *These Twain,* leaves life
in a far more impressive manner than she has ever lived it.
Her last impulse is a mean one--to cheat of her wages the
servant who even at that moment is genuinely sobbing, unnoticed, because her mistress is dying. It is not a deathbed
repentance that brings impressiveness to the death of Auntie
Hamps, but Edwin's apprehension that a person of such indomitable will must be reduced to a lump of flesh.

But in *Clayhanger* there is a further importance in Darius'
long slow dying. It means Edwin's final triumph, and for an
Edwin who could not succeed in mastering his father in the
pride of the old man's strength, there is a fascination, a form
of sexual shudder, in the spectacle of Darius craven, turning
to him, leaning on him for help. If it were not for the implied
struggle, Darius' death would not have force and ambivalence.

Bennett abandons all attempt, in this section, to enter into
Darius' mind. The story is a behavioristic account colored by
Edwin's awe as he sees his father slowly reduced to helplessness. But the reduction does not proceed by simple demonstration. As usual when Bennett is building for intensity, he con-
centrates his chapters at the beginnings. The first two days
after Darius' attack consume six chapters. Thereafter certain chapters denote the stages of the disease--from the day
when Darius, "laid aside, " surrenders the keys and power of
attorney; to the evening when he is unable to cut the sausage;
to "The Journey Upstairs"; to the final struggle "After the

Banquet. " But mixed in with these are chapters that serve to
revolve the stage--to show the pathos, irritations, and irony
of the declension. There is Darius' sad hope that Edwin will
not give Albert the thousand pounds, as well as the pathetic
gift of the watch in gratitude for Edwin's helping Darius dress
for many months. There is Edwin's "Revenge, " when the im-
pounded irritation makes him rage at the old man who had only wanted to grow mushrooms in the basement. And there are
the scenes that give perspective to Edwin's vision of his father, the father whom he has hated, such as the one where he
sees, in Big James's decision never to sing again after Darius' illness, that his own is not the universal view of Darius Clayhanger.

After the death of the founder of the Clayhanger line, the
book never finds an equally impressive motif. Osmond Orgreave, taste mediator and architect, is still important, it is
true, but the relation between the Orgreave family and Edwin had been defined in the early chapters of *Clayhanger,* and
the latter third of the book serves, as do *Hilda Lessways* and
*These Twain,* merely to redefine and emphasize it. True, the
latter third of the book consummates the romance between
Hilda and Edwin. But Hilda, though she is baffling to Edwin,
does not attain the three-dimensional quality she later captures
in *Hilda Lessways*; and as it is Edwin's side of the love story
that is stressed in the latter third of *Clayhanger,* the book suffers in proportion to our lack of interest in Edwin's passion.
Like Marcel's, it is Edwin's fate to be interesting only as a
spectator at the crises of others; and just as Marcel is more
accurate as a mirror for the love story of Swann and Odette
than as the lover of Albertine, so Edwin is never so perceptive
when suffering his own love as he is as a *voyeur* at his father's
degradation or, in *These Twain,* at Hilda's and George's meeting in Dartmoor Prison.

It remains for *Hilda Lessways* to tell a love story that has
importance, and then we see the story through Hilda's eyes.
It is not Edwin who emerges as the convincing lover, but
George Cannon.

# 7. *Hilda Lessways*

BOTH George Cannon and Hilda, the two protagonists in *Hil-da Lessways*, are *rising* characters. Hilda in particular combines some of the traits which are peculiarly Bennett's. She has an instinct for experience equaled only by Sophia's in *The Old Wives' Tale*; she has Bennett's own distrust of domesticity, and his growing impatience with provincialism; but she has also sensibility, and complicated emotions which are beyond Anna or even Sophia. She has Sophia's pride and her drive coupled with superior apprehension of the nuances of a situation.

I

And George Cannon is, for Bennett, in some respects a more sympathetic figure than Edwin. He has the drive of Bennett's beloved Denry the Audacious; he has charm, and he has decisiveness--almost all the qualities of a Bennett hero. But he lacks taste, and that is his doom. For at no time more clearly than during his writing of the Clayhanger trilogy did Bennett feel taste and the "right tone" to be so necessary an attribute of the hero. George Cannon is doomed by his obtuseness, if indeed he were not already by the plot of *Clayhanger*, which implicates him.

Hilda falls in love with George Cannon because he represents, to her undisciplined taste, a kind of culture mediator. Measured by the yardstick of the Five Towns he is a gentleman. He has a gentleman's white hands and "white wristbands, in a district where starched linen was usually either grey or bluish. " (Bennett considered white hands peculiarly the hallmark of taste. His first wife, Marguerite, says: "I first noticed his hands. They were extremely white and *soignées*. Their shape was fine. The hand of an artist, and of a man who valued the precious gift Heaven had offered him, and who knew how to take good care of that gift, " and Bennett usually reserves white hands for his favorite characters, among them Edwin's idol, Osmond Orgreave. ) George Cannon knew, too, how to wear clothes. Mrs. Lessways describes him as "the most gentlemanly man in Turnhill, and always so spruce. " He dresses well, without the provincial touch that living in Turnhill had taught Hilda to detest. His new suit has an "expensive informality" that provides a piquant contrast to his "large physical splendour. "

Hilda's first visit to his office confirms her suspicion that George Cannon is superior to other men in the Five Towns. On his desk is a copy of Victor Hugo--the same edition which her teacher, at the school "attended by girls who on the average were a little above herself in station, " had used to teach her French. Victor Hugo, the only French author whose works she knows, is Hilda's symbol of French culture.

Other impressions confirm Hilda's association of George Cannon with France. Her mother innocently remarks that Cannon is "half a foreigner . . . look at his eyes, " and events in Turnhill push the fairly commonplace hustler into a mysterious and enigmatic pose. When Hilda, virtually forgetting him, begins to be interested in Edwin, Cannon changes her mind by declaring that he is really French, and that the Five Townsmen are barbarians--a proposition that appeals to Hilda the more because she has always been ready to believe it. Cannon's declaration is caused by nothing more than pique at being pushed out of the Five Towns for operating without a solicitor's license, but it is sufficient to change the course of Hilda's life, to deflect it temporarily from Edwin Clayhanger, the conservator and good provider. For George, who turns out not to be the Real Thing, says:

"Nothing ever moves in the Five Towns. And they've

got no manners--I do believe that's the worst. Look
at Lawton's manners! Nothing but a boor! They
aren't civilized yet--that's what's the matter with
them! That's what my father used to say. Barbar-
ians, he used to say. *'Ce sont des barbares.'* . . .
Kids used to throw stones at him because of his
neck-tie. The grown-ups chuck a brick at anything
they don't quite fancy. "

That is all George says, and, ironically, he says it not from
superior sensibility, but from his chagrin. For Hilda, though,
the decisive point has been made:

Hilda saw of George Cannon all that was French in
him. She saw him quite anew, as something rather
exotic and entirely marvelous. She thought: "When
I first met him, I said to myself he was a most extraordinary man. And I was right. I was more right
than I ever imagined. No one down there has any
idea of what he really is. They're too stupid, as he
says. "
He had imposed on her his scorn of the provincial.
She had to share it. She had a vision of the Five
Towns as a smoky blotch on the remote horizon--
negligible, crass, ridiculous in its heavy self-com-
placency. The very Orgreaves themselves were
tinged with this odious English provincialism.

"The very Orgreaves . . . tinged with odious English provincialism"! Hilda is far gone, for to her, as to Edwin and to
any Five Townsman with a pretension to culture, the Orgreaves
have been undisputed arbiters of elegance. Hilda is suffering,
in her inchoate, Bennett way, from the malady that attacks
James's Strether (in *The Ambassadors*), not in Paris itself,
but in so unlikely a place as Liverpool. James's style puts
Strether on a plane that Hilda cannot hope to attain, but Strether's first apprehension of the magic of French culture and
manners is not so very different:

. . . this struck him as really, in comparison, his

introduction to things. It hadn't been "Europe" at
Liverpool, no--not even in the dreadful, delightful
streets the night before--to the extent his present
companion made it so. She had not yet done that so
much so as when, after their walk had lasted a few
minutes and he had had time to wonder if a couple
of sidelong glances from her meant that he had best
have put on gloves, she almost pulled him up with an
amused challenge, "But why--fondly as it's so easy
to imagine your clinging to it--don't you put it away?
Or if it's an inconvenience to you to carry it, one is
often glad to have one's card back. "

For even so insouciant a character as Strether, then, being
a European, being desirably French, turns on so simple a
matter as whether he had best put on his gloves, and on whether he should carry a visiting card in his hand. If James has at
times so one-dimensional a standard for taste, a semisophisticated Bennett heroine will naturally take George Cannon's French *"barbares"* as a sign that he has important insights.

But Hilda is to be disillusioned about George--and not by her
discovery that he is a bigamist. On the contrary, she reflects
that "he could have won me on any terms he liked" and again,
"it isn't all your fault. It's just as much mine as yours. . . .
After all, you took the chances. You did what you thought was
best. "

It is not his bigamy, although she knows he has "ruined"her,
that appalls Hilda. On the contrary, she regards it as a deliv-
erance: "She knew that fate had favoured her by absolving her
from the consequences of a tragic weakness and error. " Her
tragic error has been in mistaking George for a man of taste.
He never masters the nuances of manners which, to Hilda almost alone among Bennett's heroines, mean much. Whenever he lapses from taste, even during the ardor of courtship,
Hilda is uneasy: "George Cannon had not understood. He did
not feel as she felt, and her emotion was incommunicable to
him. A tremendous misgiving seized her. . . ." After their
marriage she finds that her premonition that George lacks tone
has real foundation; she is "shocked by the coarseness and the

obtuseness which evidently characterized his attitude, now as
on other occasions . . . it was ominously sinister. "

## II

Thwarted in her attempts to find a good European in George
Cannon, Hilda turns immediately to the Orgreaves, whom she
earlier deserted for George. Again she makes one of those little
Jamesian tests which are second nature to her, and when this
time the Orgreaves pass it successfully, she thinks: "George
Cannon would never have understood this. But everyone here
understands it. "

For Hilda, culture has again become bound up with the Orgreaves. There is Janet, a "well-dressed, kind-featured, and
almost beautiful young woman" who has that mark of a lady, a
"charming air of diffidence. "Again she is Hilda's best friend,
replacing George Cannon's sister, the dancing mistress, who
until she narrows down into a boardinghouse keeper has,
through her mastery of the elegancies of French deportment,
justified Hilda's childlike devotion to her.  There is still Osmond, founder of the family culture and Edwin's mentor. And,
as a substitute for George, there is Edwin Clayhanger, whom
Hilda had met first at the Orgreaves', and with whom she now
urgently renews her intrigue.  Edwin is "clever" and "would
have wealth and importance and reputation" as she has earlier
reflected in a girlish revery. Moreover, he has what she sought
and missed in George, "an exotic and wistful quality which
neither she nor anyone else could possibly define. " But this
much definition she might give it: it is not the look of Darius
Clayhanger, whom she thinks "a fat, untidy old man, " fit only
to be bundled off somewhere where his bad manners will not
show. It is the look of the conservator; it is the "romantic
visage, wistful, full of sad subtleties, of the unknown and the
seductive, " that she had first seen from the railway carriage,
and whose story Janet Orgreave summed up in a few words--
the story not of Edwin Clayhanger alone, but of second generations: "He wanted to be an architect. That was how father got
to know him. But old Mr. Clayhanger wouldn't have it. And
so he's a printer, and one day he'll be one of the principal
men in the town. "

## III

*Hilda Lessways* is Jamesian in its limited point of view and even more so in covering, from a slightly different angle, the same ground as *Clayhanger*--reminiscent, in this double focus, of *The Golden Bowl* and *The Wings of the Dove*. The story is seen now through the eyes of Hilda. She is not, like Edwin, a second-generation child. She is the granddaughter of the founder of her line, Grandfather Lessways, a teapot manufacturer. Her removal from the source of the family fortune has perhaps made her more the artist, or at least the dilettante, than conservator Edwin. At the beginning of the story Hilda is a woman with property. She and her mother own Lessways Street and the Freehold Villas. They have many tenants. Furthermore, her house has some pretensions to superiority, "some faint traces of Georgian amenity. "

The opening scenes, which define Hilda's relations to her mother, recall the uneasy yet intimate companionship of the women in *The Old Wives' Tale*. Perhaps Bennett himself is most aware that he repeats some strategies of the earlier novel. There is a touch of self-consciousness in: "The domestic existence of unmated women together, though it is full of secret exasperations, also has its hours of charm--a charm honied, perverse, and unique. " But if Mrs. Lessways is an inferior old Constance, Hilda is by no means a lesser young Sophia. She has capacities for experience that she shares with Sophia, but she has an enlarged talent for tiny discriminations, a sensibility not Sophia's, and a deeper thirst for culture. Bennett tells us that even as a child, Hilda had been willful, but "supercilious. " And as she grows older, small lapses from taste, such as the red flannel wrapped around her mother's head when she had a cold, are "offensive and ridiculous" to her. She hates, too, the "confined and stifling circle of domestic dailiness. " Hilda is pained by her mother's undignified plan to collect her own rents. She resolves that she will not permit it (significantly, this resolution first persuades her to visit the law offices of George Cannon). Hilda Lessways despises provincialism from the time she can talk, whereas Sophia comes to hate it only as a result of her years in Paris.

Crucial episodes in Hilda's culture adventure are selling the family home and properties on her mother's death, at which she is not present because she felt it more important to help George Cannon at the newspaper office than to attend her mother's illness--and entrusting her fortune to George Cannon. George's victory over Hilda's mother is significant, for Mrs. Lessways is a Constance-like, reactionary character, and George an apostle of adventure and of foreign glamour. In selling her properties, Hilda feels that she is breaking with the Five Towns, and that henceforth she will be a woman of independent means and free will.

Her next choice becomes whether to remain with the Orgreaves or to follow George. As I have shown, because of the *"ce sont des barbares"* episode she chooses to follow George to Brighton. At Brighton the story takes on a third dimension; these chapters are the best in the novel because here we see not only Brighton as it looks to Hilda, but George as he presently looks against the backdrop of Brighton--and, in retrospect, the Five Towns' Edwin and George, as they look to a Brighton-initiated Hilda. The section has some of the ambivalence achieved in the Paris section of *The Old Wives' Tale*. Like Sophia, Hilda has made a pilgrimage, even if not to Paris. At Brighton she comes to understand that the Cannons' culture is synthetic, that they do not have the right manner, and she turns again to the Orgreave family which had symbolized culture for Edwin Clayhanger. The Orgreaves reintroduce Edwin into Hilda's life, but she cannot at once accept his love, because she is carrying George Cannon's child. She goes into hiding at Brighton, and emerges only after a long interval as the returned exile, like Sophia, to marry Edwin, conservator of the Clayhanger fortune.

## IV

Why, though Hilda of *Hilda Lessways* is more complex than the Edwin of *Clayhanger,* and though George Cannon is at least as interesting as Edwin and in some respects more so, is the second book of the trilogy inferior to the first? Principally because it lacks the tenseness of the two-level conflict. There is no Darius Clayhanger to battle with the Orgreaves for Hilda's soul. Her adventure is presented more as a pilgrimage, in which she stands for a time at the crossroads, and tries first one road and then the other. The first leads her to George Cannon, and the second to Edwin. But both George and Edwin are, in their way, on the side of Bennett's angels.

However, out of *Hilda Lessways* emerges the heroine who is the most complex Bennett was capable of drawing, who shows most clearly the direction he was traveling when his developing love for power and money gradually deflected his interest toward less ambivalent and narrower protagonists. For Hilda is a woman with all the drive of a Sophia Baines, but with something more. She suggests in Bennett a hitherto undeveloped talent for nuances. Even in *The Old Wives' Tale*, Bennett could seldom resist the tendency to simplify and cap with an epigram the emotions of his characters. In the scene, for example, where Sophia wonders why she refused to marry the balloonist, Bennett reduces what had promised to be a Mannian set of ambiguities to a one-level summing up. But in *Hilda Lessways,* Bennett has progressed beyond the need to codify. When Miss Gailey is about to drown herself, and Hilda has run out frantically to stop her: '"Please do come back with me!' Hilda implored; but she spoke mechanically, as though saying something which she was bound to say, but which she did not feel."

There is perceptible ambiguity in the scene in which George Cannon first brings Hilda to the Brighton boardinghouse, and in the scene in which she learns that she is married to a bigamist. In the latter scene, she objects not so much to the fact that George *is* a bigamist, as to his manner of revealing the fact:

> "I'm ashamed!" he said, without reserve, abasing himself. "I'm utterly ashamed. I'd give anything to be able to undo it. "
>
> She was startled and offended. She had not expected that he would kiss the dust. . . .
>
> "Of course, " he said, after a pause, "I'm completely done for!"
>
> He spoke so solemnly, and with such intense conviction, that she was awed and appalled. She felt as one who, having alone escaped destruction in an

earthquake, stands afar off and contemplates the
silent, corpse-strewn ruin of a vast city.

It is with such unexpected insights that Bennett, in *Hilda
Lessways*, goes beyond *The Old Wives' Tale*, and even, to
some extent, *Clayhanger*. No one would pretend that it has the
stature of the two better books, but it has its own excellences,
and they are those of taste and perception. Bennett was pro-
ceeding haltingly in the directions of James and Forster. But
he had a long way to travel, and he was tiring of the road.

# 8. *These Twain*

AT THE opening of *These Twain,* Edwin has become the conservator that his surrender to his father's will in Book I of
*Clayhanger* foreshadowed. He has inherited, along with the
printing business, a growing obsession with the problems of
his trade. But, though he fancies himself the bearded head
of a clan, and is given to reflections such as that he is "getting accustomed to power and dominion . . . Albert would
have to knuckle down to him, and Clara too, " he is actually
still less the source than the vessel, and he is still fought over
by representatives of competing views of life: the architect's
and the printer's. The remnants of the Orgreaves now carry
on the battle against the surviving Clayhangers. The growing
influence of the printing business makes Edwin waver toward
the orbit of the Clayhangers, and it is again the mission of the
Orgreaves, led now by Hilda, to win him back.

*These Twain* shows Hilda in a new position which, rein-
forced by that of the commentator, Tertius Ingpen, is the new
position of Bennett himself. The book reflects Bennett's increasing preoccupation with the unpleasant aspects of provincialism, and increasing conviction that the battle for culture cannot be fought out in the Five Towns. It follows that Edwin was wrong in choosing printer over architect; and his
wrongness is underlined and emphasized when, in *These Twain,*
he wants to prevent George Cannon, his stepson, from going
to London and becoming the architect his own father had prevented him from being:

Hilda had told him that during the visit to London
the project for articling George to Johnnie Orgreave
had been revived, but she had not said that a decision
had been taken. Though Edwin from careful pride
had not spoken freely--George being Hilda's affair
and not his--he had shown no enthusiasm . . . he
did not at all care for George going to London. Why
should it be thought necessary for George to go to
London? The sagacious and successful provincial
in Edwin was darkly jealous of London, as a rival
superficial and brilliant. And now he learnt from
Ingpen that George's destiny was fixed.

Edwin had reflected in *Clayhanger* that it was "absurd and
scandalous that he had never been to London: he ought for his
self-respect to depart thither at once." London had once been
almost as meaningful for him as Paris for Sophia Baines. But
now Hilda has to struggle to get him out of Bursley, before he
becomes even more Darius-like; *These Twain* is built upon this
struggle. The first book, in which she tries to prevent Edwin
from expanding the business, is made up of several pitched
battles between her side and the Clayhangers. Hilda wins the
opening skirmishes, but loses the crucial battle which ends
the first book. An analysis of a few of these skirmishes will
show the essential conflict.

I

Book I is built into large units, each of which symbolizes
some phase of the clash between the opposing groups. The
opening scenes, at the housewarming, define the battle lines.
The Orgreave faction, made up of Hilda, Janet Orgreave and
her brothers, and Tertius Ingpen, cluster in the living room
for an evening of talk and music, while the Clayhanger faction,
composed of Maggie, Clara, Albert, Auntie Hamps, and the
Wesleyan Methodist minister, cluster conspiratorially in the
kitchen. Edwin wavers between the two camps, now irritated
with his wife because she is not cordial enough to the Clayhangers, now resenting the fact that Darius' survivors will
not mix with the Orgreaves, still not sure where he belongs.

Hilda's group wins the two opening skirmishes, and for a time succeeds in identifying Edwin's interests with its own. The initial skirmish is caused by Mrs. Hamps's effort to involve Edwin in Wesleyan church politics--first by getting the minister to invite Edwin to act as district treasurer of the Fund, and second by begging Edwin to retain the family pew. Edwin delights Hilda by having the courage to refuse the treasurership, though she independently endorses his refusal with, "Oh, no! I won't have it. " But in the matter of the pew, Hilda is the independent agent for protecting Edwin:

> "Now, Auntie, " the tingling woman warned Auntie
> Hamps as one powerful individuality may warn an-
> other, "don't worry about us. You know we're not
> great chapel-goers. " . . .
> Edwin knew that she detested Auntie Hamps. Aun-
> tie Hamps no doubt also knew it. In their mutual
> smilings, so affable, so hearty, so appreciative, ap-
> parently so impulsive, the hostility between them
> gleamed mysteriously like lightning in sunlight.
> "Mrs. Edwin's family were Church of England, "
> said Auntie Hamps, in the direction of Mr. Peartree.
> "Not great church-goers, either, " Hilda finished
> cheerfully.
> No woman had ever made such outrageous re-
> marks in the Five Towns before. . . . Both Mrs.
> Hamps and the minister thought that Hilda was not
> going the right way to live down her dubious past.
> Even Edwin in his pride was flurried. Great matters,
> however had been accomplished. . . . A word said,
> bravely, in a particular tone--and a new epoch was
> begun. The pity was that he had not done it all him-
> self. Hilda's courage had surpassed his own.

The second triumph of the Orgreave faction, also bound up intimately with an escape from the domination of the church, is implicit in Hilda's decision that regular Sunday evening concerts will be held at their house. This decision, backed by Janet and Johnnie Orgreave, Tertius Ingpen, and even Edwin himself, is a momentous one. The Sunday evening musicales are a direct defiance of the church's domination over the Five Towns:

> The Sunday musical evening, beyond its artistic thrills and emotional quality, proved to be exciting as a social manifestation. Those present at it felt as must feel Russian conspirators in a back room of some big grey house of a Petrograd suburb when the secret printing-press begins to function before their eyes. This concert of profane harmonies, deliberately planned and pouring out through open windows to affront the ears of returners from church and chapel, was considered by its organizers as a remarkable event; and rightly so. The Clayhanger house might have been a fortress, with a blood-red standard of art and freedom floating from a pole lashed to its chimney.

Hilda is the organizer, the initiator of this excursion into culture. Toward her Mrs. Hamps indignantly directs the attack which comes in "The Family at Home," a chapter which demonstrates the fundamental cleavage between the two factions:

> "We're having a little music on Sunday night," said Hilda, as it were apologetically, and scorning herself for being apologetic. Why should she be apologetic to these base creatures? But she couldn't help it; the public opinion of the room was too strong for her. She even added: "We're hoping that old Mrs. Orgreave will come. It will be the first time she's been out in the evening for ever so long." The name of Mrs. Orgreave was calculated by Hilda to overawe them and stop their mouths.
>
> No name, however, could overawe Mrs. Hamps. She smiled kindly, and with a respect for the caprices of others; she spoke in a tone exceptionally polite--but what she said was: "I'm sorry . . . I'm sorry."
>
> The deliverance was final.

At this rebuke from Mrs. Hamps, Hilda reflects on how as-
tonishing it is that Edwin should be so very different from the
other Clayhangers. And then: "But after all, was he? She could
see in him sometimes bits of Maggie, of Clara, and even of
the Unspeakable. She was conscious of her grievances against
Edwin."

Hilda is soon to have more grievances. Her alliance with
the Orgreaves has been her greatest strength against the Clayhangers, but at the end of Book I that alliance suffers an ab-
rupt check in the death of both Mr. and Mrs. Orgreave, within
twenty-four hours of each other. This calamity is recognizable
as a variation of Bennett's device for defeating the architect
at the end of Book I of *Clayhanger*: for the funeral of the Or-
greaves--its lack of pomp and of support from the town's people, and the subsequent discovery that Osmond Orgreave had
died penniless--does much to weaken the hold of the architect
on Edwin:

> Except for the matter of the Palace Porcelain
> Company, Edwin was not surprised at the revela-
> tions, though he tried to be. The more closely he
> examined his attitude for years past to the Orgreave
> household structure, the more clearly he had to ad-
> mit that a suspicion of secret financial rottenness
> had never been absent from his mind--not even at
> the period of renewed profuseness, a year or two
> ago, when furniture-dealers, painters, and paper-
> hangers had been enriched. His resentment against
> the deceased charming Osmond and also against the
> affectionate and blandly confident mother, was keen
> and cold.

The other half of Edwin's grievance against the Orgreaves
is that they had "existed, morally, on Janet for many years;
monopolized her, absorbed her, aged her, worn her out," and
these two grievances are enough to diminish Edwin's fascination with problems of taste that had been revived by Hilda's two
successes in the opening chapters of *These Twain*. During
Books II and III Edwin comes more and more under the influence of the printing faction, and it is only at the end of

Book III that he yields to Hilda's command that they move
from the Five Towns before they are wholly debased by their
influence. In what amounts to Bennett's farewell to the Five
Towns, Edwin has a long soliloquy:

> The Orgreaves had gone, and had been succeeded
> by excellent people with whom it was impossible to
> fraternize. There were rumours that in view of Tom
> Swetnam's imminent defection the Swetnam house-
> hold might be broken up and the home abandoned.
> The Suttons, now that Beatrice Sutton had left the
> district, talked seriously of going. Only Dr. Stir-
> ling was left on that side of the road, and he stayed
> because he must. The once exclusive Terraces on
> the other side were losing their quality. Old Darius
> Clayhanger had risen out of the mass, but he was
> fiercely exceptional. Now the whole mass seemed
> to be rising, under the action of some strange leaven,
> and those few who by intelligence, by manners, or
> by money counted themselves select were fleeing
> as from an inundation.
>   Edwin had not meant to join the exodus. But he
> too would join it. Destiny had seized him. Let him
> be as democratic in spirit as he would, his fate was
> to be cut off from the democracy, with which, for
> the rest, he had very little of speech or thought, or
> emotion in common, but in which, from an impla-
> cable sense of justice, he was religiously and un-
> changeably determined to put his trust.

*These Twain* was the last book Bennett wrote about the Five
Towns. His solution for Edwin is, of course, a compromise.
Edwin's defeat by Darius at the end of Book I of *Clayhanger*
had made an exile to London, like Bennett's, impossible. Instead, Edwin takes one of the two extremely important alternatives which are presented in Book II of *These Twain*.

II

At the end of Book I, Hilda has received two definite checks.

The Orgreaves are in sudden eclipse, and Edwin has decided
to devote more time to the printing business. Hilda yields to
this decision only when she discovers her son, George, drawing a picture that announces his intention of becoming an architect.

> "What is he drawing, this kid?" asked Edwin,
> genially. . . . The first thing he noticed was some
> lettering, achieved in an imitation of architect's
> lettering: "Plan for proposed new printing-works
> to be erected by Edwin Clayhanger, Esq., upon
> land at Shawport. George Edwin Clayhanger, Ar-
> chitect." . . . and here was exposed the secret and
> the result of his chumminess with Johnnie Orgreave.
> . . .
>
> Hilda, behind the back of proud, silent George,
> pulled Edwin's face to her and kissed it. . . . Her
> eyes seemed to be saying: "Have your works; I have
> yielded. Perhaps it is George's plan that has made
> me yield. . . ."

The defeat is absolute. Hilda definitely abandons the fight
against printing, as Edwin does at the end of Book I of *Clayhanger*. George will be her architect. But, like Osmond Orgreave in Books II and III of *Clayhanger*, Hilda still has plans
to save Edwin's spirit, if not his body.

Book II, concerned with the growing Clayhanger influence on
Edwin, opens with the Darius survivors in renewed battle for
Edwin. First Clara and her children, and then Auntie Hamps,
visit Edwin at his enlarged printing works--enlarged at their
instigation. Auntie Hamps is doubly triumphant. First, because, as Darius' sister and the only survivor of the older
generation, she is witnessing Darius' triumph over his re-
captured son: '"I must say, Edwin'--she looked round the small
office and seemed to be looking round the whole works in a superb glance--'you make me proud of you. You make me proud
to be your auntie'"; and second, because she is able to an-
nounce the downfall of Johnnie Orgreave, Osmond Orgreave's
son and successor as architect, who has run away with a Mrs.
Chris Hansom. Her reaction is significant:

He was a friend, and a close friend, of all three
of them--Hilda, Edwin, and Tertius Ingpen. . . .
He had shamed them, irretrievably lowered their
prestige. They could not look Auntie Hamps in the
face. But Auntie Hamps could look them in the face.
And her glance, charged with grief and satisfaction,
said: "How are the mighty fallen, with their jaunty
parade of irreligion, and their musical evenings on
Sunday, with the windows open while folks are coming home from chapel!" And there could be no re-
tort.

The second scene of Book II presents Hilda's strategic retreat from Mrs. Hamps, in a pilgrimage to Tavy Mansion.
This pilgrimage occupies the remainder of Book II, and presents the two alternatives which face those who escape from
an industrial civilization like the Five Towns: manners, and
primitivism. The locale, significantly, is the mansion home
of Alicia Orgreave, now Mrs. Hesketh. The first of these alternatives presents itself to Hilda as the only possible one, and
it is the one she finally forces Edwin to choose, a retreat from
the Five Towns to a country mansion of tradition and authority,
where one can live the Orgreave life. Hilda is enamored of
Tavy Mansion:

These people lived in lovely and cleanly surroundings without a care . . . they were well-bred, and
they were attended by servants who, professionally,
were even better bred than themselves . . . they
had absolutely no problems . . . their world was
ideal . . . whereas Hilda and hers were forced to
live among a brutal populace, amid the most horri-
ble surroundings of smoke, dirt, and squalor. In
Devonshire the Five Towns was unthinkable. . . .
And compare . . . even the old garden of the Orgreaves, with this elysium, where nothing offended
the eye and the soot nowhere lay on the trees, black-
ening the shiny leaves and stunting the branches. . . .

The second alternative to Five Towns industrialism presents

itself, significantly, to Edwin when he comes to Tavy Mansion
to fetch Hilda. As he drives through the Devonshire wilds with
the Orgreaves, he has his first apprehension of the second of
two alternatives that offer escapes from the Five Towns:

> Edwin, in the body of the wagonette with Janet
> and Alicia, looked for hut-circles and saw none;
> but he did not care. He was content with the knowl-
> edge that prehistoric hut-circles were somewhere
> there. He had never seen wild England before, and
> its primeval sanity awoke in him the primeval man.
> The healthiness and simplicity and grandiose beauty
> of it created the sublime illusion that civilization
> was worthy to be abandoned. The Five Towns seemed
> intolerable by their dirt and ugliness, and by the
> tedious intricacy of their existence. Lithography,
> --you had but to think of the word to perceive the
> paltriness of the thing! Riches, properties, pro-
> prieties, all the safeties, --futile! He could have
> lived alone with Hilda on the moor, begetting chil-
> dren by her, watching with satisfaction the growing
> curves of her fecundity--his work . . . he had a
> tremendous, a painful longing for such a life . . .
> he felt that he had never before peered into the depths
> of existence . . . he seemed to guess that beneath
> the tiresome surfaces of life in the Five Towns the
> essence of it might be mystically lived.

These two alternatives present themselves also to Ru-
dolph Birkin in *Women in Love*: Breadalby, owned by the
woman of taste, Hermione, and primitivism, represented
by Ursula, daughter of a farmer with many children. But
Lawrence's primitivism means receptivity to "life" and to
revolt from English society, whereas Bennett's means merely escape from the "tedious intricacy" of the social organization.

Edwin toys, then, with the idea of becoming a primitive on
the D. H. Lawrence pattern, or at least the E. M. Forster.
But Hilda has other plans, as Bennett himself had. Bennett
never went the primitive road. His choice for himself was a ,

combination of Hilda's and Edwin's: a country estate, and increasing preoccupation with his business. And a third choice,
which presents itself to Hilda in Book III of *These Twain*--
flight to London--was Bennett's choice, also. After *These
Twain* he never turned to Five Towns again, even in his books.

### III

The end of Book II finds Hilda in a second eclipse. Thwarted
in her attempts to gain at least the illusion of a renewed romance with George Cannon (her trip to Tavy Mansion includes
a side trip to Dartmoor Prison where George is incarcerated,
and her desire to be the instrument of his release is frustrated
by Edwin's superior generosity in giving him the money to
escape to America), Hilda reflects that she no longer has free
will, that she is wholly at the mercy of Edwin's Clayhanger
money. This predicament has been Edwin's at the end of Book
II of *Clayhanger*, except that there it is Darius who controls
the money, and prevents Edwin's alliance with Hilda, as Edwin now prevents Hilda's spiritual alliance with George Cannon.
(In every way the over-all structure of *These Twain* follows
that of *Clayhanger*.) Hilda longs for London, that symbol which
had appealed to Edwin in the days of his captivity to Darius:
"She was a captive, and she recalled with a gentle pang . . .
the days when she was unhappy and free as a man, when she
could say, 'I will go to London,' 'I will leave London,' 'I am
deceived and ruined, but I am my own mistress.'"
Book III finds Hilda fulfilling her wish, over Edwin's express
and bitter opposition. She does go to London, and directly to
the Orgreaves, on the pretext that her architect son, George,
is having trouble with his eyes. Charlie Orgreave can recom-
mend a good oculist (Charlie saved George's life in Book III
of *Clayhanger*, when Hilda made a similar determined pilgrimage to London). This, the second pilgrimage of *These Twain*,
marks the beginning of Hilda's ascendancy over Edwin, the
downfall of the Darius survivors, climaxed in Edwin's soliloquy when he decides to move to a country home. For in London Hilda discovers that the "Orgreave Calamity" which brings
Book I to its dramatic close has been only a Five Towns
eclipse. In London their star shines more brightly than ever.

This discovery is crucial to an understanding of Bennett's last books, as well as to a clear vision of the "message" of the Clayhanger trilogy:

> She discovered Charlie Orgreave, the fairly success-
> ful doctor in Ealing (a suburb rich in doctors), to be
> the perfect Londoner, and Janet, no longer useless
> and forlorn, scarcely less so. These two, indeed,
> had the air of having at length reached their proper
> home *after being born in exile.* [Italics mine.] The
> same was true of Johnnie Orgreave, now safely
> through the matrimonial court and married to his
> blonde Adela, the ripping Mrs. Chris Hansom, whose
> money had bought him a junior partnership in an
> important architectural firm in Russell Square. . . . .
> The current Five Towns notion of Johnnie and his
> wife as two morally crushed creatures hiding for the
> rest of their lives in shame from an outraged pub-
> lic opinion, seemed merely comic in Ealing and
> Bedford Park. These people referred to the Five
> Towns with negligent affection, but with disdain, as
> to a community that, with all its good qualities, had
> not yet emerged from barbarism . . . when she
> mentioned that she hoped soon to move Edwin into
> a country house, they applauded and implied that no
> other course was possible.

This, except for Edwin's soliloquy, is Bennett's last word on the subject of the Five Towns. The Orgreaves' restoration is complete. Mrs. Hamps is triumphant in the Five Towns-- her funeral, structurally contrasted with that of Osmond Or- greave, is far more costly and better attended by the towns- people, including the important bank manager, while Osmond's is small and unattended. The Hamps's opinion of Johnnie Or- greave's elopement has become the settled opinion of Bursley, and Janet is regarded as a hopeless old maid. But in London the Orgreave tribe, having fled from the Five Towns, has tri- umphed. Johnnie is the successful architect, and will do for George Cannon what his father Osmond had never been able to do for Edwin: save him from the printing business and the Five

Towns. Charlie is a successful doctor, though his father died penniless in Bursley. And Janet, the Bursley old maid, is in London "no longer useless and forlorn." Only Tom Orgreave, remaining in Bursley, violates the Orgreave code by becoming a miser. The "message" of *These Twain* is the message of the exile: the battle for taste must and will be fought--but not in the Five Towns.

Some of the themes of the last Bennett novels are suggested in *These Twain*. Hilda's feeling that a partial solution to the Edwin predicament might be political activity, hints at *Lord Raingo*; and the country house is Bennett's own solution to relieving the pressure of increasing business. (Both the house and its corollary, the yacht, are important in Bennett's last books, as is the man preoccupied with his business--notably in *Imperial Palace*.) And the primitive worship of woman as *mother*, never seen in Bennett before *These Twain* (Minnie, Auntie Hamps's pregnant servant; and the mothers Alicia, Hilda, and Clara), foreshadows Bennett's indulgent attitude toward Lilian in the novel of that title. Tension between primitivism and taste, characteristic of the books in which Bennett was convinced the battle for taste could be waged in the Five Towns, does not reappear.

IV

It has become an established cliché to speak of the third book of the Clayhanger trilogy as largely autobiographical, a series of petty quarrels in which nothing significant is at stake, a naturalistic account of the adjustments of Bennett and his first wife. Nothing could be farther from the facts of Bennett's careful construction, but until the significance of the themes of *Clayhanger* and *Hilda Lessways* has been grasped, there is no key to the quarrels in *These Twain*. While they doubtless make use of autobiographical details, their meaning in the structure of the trilogy goes beyond the private adjustments of Arnold and Marguerite.

The theme of *These Twain* is that of "The Buried Question of Domicile" section of *The Old Wives' Tale*, with a different emphasis given by different characters and a shifting set of values. Edwin is a male Constance, a conservator, who wants to remain in Bursley and carry on the role in which he has been cast by circumstances and temperament. Hilda is a Sophia, who, as returned exile with a taste for the larger perspectives she has left behind, wants to escape to the place of her initiation and to carry with her the beloved person with whom she is involved, without whom life would be unimaginable. But though there are marked resemblances between the Sophia-Constance and the Hilda-Edwin clashes over the question of what Five Townsmen called a "flitting," the problem has become enormously complicated in *These Twain* by a factor which does not enter into the clash between Constance and Sophia. *These Twain* has for its protagonists two characters farther up on the cultural curve than the Baines sisters: Hilda and Edwin are culture seekers for whom the question of domicile is more complex than it is for an Anna or a Sophia. By the time of *These Twain*, a much more complex set of manners and cultural values is at stake for those who remain in Bursley.

Therefore Bennett's solution to the whole problem is different. Whereas in *The Old Wives' Tale* he permits Constance to triumph over Sophia in the matter of changing homes, in *These Twain* it is Hilda who triumphs over Edwin, with Bennett's qualified blessing. He still has respect for the conservator, the Constance or the Edwin or even the Samuel Povey. But his respect has become tempered, in the years that separate *The Old Wives' Tale* from *These Twain*, by a growing estrangement from the Five Towns, and a growing impatience with the provincial rejection of the architect in favor of the printer. Another element enters into the new picture. Bennett's sympathy is divided, in *Clayhanger*, between the dominant, aggressive Darius and the recessive, artistic Edwin. He has sympathy for Edwin's ambitions, but respect for Darius' power. The shift in position in *These Twain* further complicates the problem. Mild Edwin has now taken the place of aggressive Darius, and is attempting to follow him in personality as well as in the printing shop. Bennett is fully aware of the ironies implicit in this shift. But the Edwin-Darius of *These Twain* does not have as his housemate the meek son of *Clayhanger*, but Hilda, the aggressive, dominant, and still culture-seeking woman Edwin chose in the first book of the trilogy.

The problem can best be made explicit by an examination
of the attitude of Tertius Ingpen, who in *These Twain* sup-
plants Osmond Orgreave as a culture symbol and who acts as
the mediator between Edwin and Hilda. Tertius is a typical
Bennett-realized symbol of the man of taste who is supposed
to give a certain perspective to the viewpoints of the main
characters (who are always on a lower cultural level than Bennett himself has achieved). Tertius, introduced at the opening
of Book I of *These Twain,* at the housewarming, is recognizable
at once as one of the figures--now Dr. Stirling, now the Suttons or the Orgreaves--who in several Bennett novels serve
to give Five Towns people a point of reference to the world
outside:

> He was a native of the district, having been born
> somewhere in the aristocratic regions between Knype
> and the lordly village of Sneyd, but what first struck
> the local observer in him was that his speech had
> none of the local accent. In the pursuit of his voca-
> tion he has lived in other places than the Five Towns.
> For example, in London, where he had become
> acquainted with Edwin's friend, Charlie Orgreave,
> the doctor. When Ingpen received a goodish ap-
> pointment amid the industrial horrors of his birth,
> Charlie Orgreave recommended him to Edwin, and
> Edwin and Ingpen had met once, under arrangement
> made by Johnnie Orgreave. It was Johnnie who had
> impulsively suggested in Ingpen's presence that Ing-
> pen should be invited to the At Home.

We recognize the familiar signs: Tertius has none of the
local accent, though a native of the Five Towns; therefore he
is from the towns but not of them; and he has been introduced
into the Clayhanger circle under the Orgreave aegis. We know
therefore that we are to take his opinion seriously. And it is
precisely this that provides the ambivalence that is *These
Twain*'s most outstanding quality. For though in matters of
culture--books, music, the selection of a place to live--Ter-
tius is on the side of Hilda, he takes Edwin's part on the question of whether he or Hilda shall dominate. He feels that Hilda

is right, but that Edwin as a man ought in justice to prevail. And that is what gives the slightly blurred focus to *These Twain*. Bennett, too, is on Hilda's side of the culture clash; as I have shown, he is never unequivocal in his statement that the Five Towns must be tempered by some sort of cultural pilgrimage; but he is with Tertius in feeling that Edwin should be the man of the family. He is artist enough to perceive, however, that having married an Edwin to a Hilda, he cannot expect to wrench their love story into a cozy tale of domesticity, with Edwin as strong provider and Hilda as womanly leaner. He is true to his original conception of Edwin in having him bow to the stronger will of Hilda, just as he did to Darius in *Clayhanger*. The paradox is that while, in bowing to Darius, Edwin yields to the enemy of the architect, in bowing to Hilda he yields to the friend of the Orgreaves and the still loyal champion of taste. But there remains a note of exasperation detectable in Bennett's attitude toward Hilda!

# 9. Craftsmanlike Realism

WITH THE establishment of the surviving Orgreaves in London and the enlisting of young George Cannon in the army, the last architects disappear from Bennett's novels. The card and the millionaire join to conquer the world as they had been threatening to do from the first. The combination of sympathies which had made it possible for Bennett to mediate between the certainties of the middle class and rising new aspirations disintegrates. Just as Bennett ceases in the *Journal* to be concerned with literature and becomes the recorder of evenings spent with earls and actresses, the complex planes of the earlier novels merge into one level, presenting a frankly *nouveau riche* point of view. *The Pretty Lady, Lilian, Lord Raingo,* and *Imperial Palace* are all positive statements of this point of view, and all have only one real level. *Riceyman Steps,* though better, is the obverse--the realistic portrayal, by some of the tricks of the earlier novels, of the miser, the supreme antispeculator, the temperamental enemy of the card, and Bennett's clearest representation of inhibition.

A great deal of exaggeration has entered into estimates of Bennett's later novels. They are inferior to *The Old Wives' Tale* and the Clayhanger trilogy, but, if the comparison is with *Leonora* or *Sacred and Profane Love,* or *A Man from the North,* the case is less clear. *Riceyman Steps* and *Lord Raingo* are competent realistic novels. They are honest in a way that *Leonora* and *Sacred and Profane Love* are not, and they have

far better craftsmanship than *A Man from the North,* or than
*Anna of the Five Towns.*

Nevertheless, by the standards of Bennett's best work--
*The Old Wives' Tale,* the Clayhanger trilogy, and *Anna of the
Five Towns*--the later novels show a narrowing of conception
and characterization. In his five best novels Bennett is concerned with a whole world of characters separated and brought
together by their tastes and aspirations; the possibilities for
interaction are great, and Bennett builds a complex structure
and symbolism. The two best of his later novels have fewer
characters and fewer meaningful attitudes.

*Riceyman Steps* deals with the psychology of the crudest form
of asceticism--miserliness so strong that it starves both the
miser and his victim. Henry Earlforward is literally a miser,
but miserliness, as it appears in Earlforward's relations
with his wife, and as it grows into an obsession, becomes
a symbol that gives the novel force. The development of the
obsession, in particular, makes the work seem of contemporary relevance and probably accounts for its recent reissue.
(L. P. Hartley might have conceived the general structure.)
But Bennett's ability to show the literal existence of miserliness is greater than his ability to expand the symbolic meanings. As actual misers Earlforward and Mrs. Arb are sometimes so real that they seem to embarrass Bennett into jokes
about things that are not jokes. He tries so hard to stand away
from his realism that he loses some of the effect of the obsession. His banter, successful in the earlier novels, here often looks like an uncomfortable defense against identifying too
closely with a trait that, in his other view of himself as a man
of wealth, he finds almost a subject for satire.

By the time of *Riceyman Steps* Bennett had acquired whatever sophistication he was going to and had lost his resentment against the particular restrictions of life in the Five
Towns. He turns his considerable talent for writing about restrictiveness to an adult and metropolitan theme. *Riceyman
Steps* suggests a potentiality, never wholly fulfilled, for developing a serious novel different from *Clayhanger* or *The Old
Wives' Tale.* In it more than in any of the other novels, the
hero alone is directly responsible for his difficulties.

The structure develops from a comic portrayal of absurdity

to a pathetic picture of neglected and wasted effort. Earlforward progresses from a successful, bachelor miser to a married hunger artist perfecting his talent almost to the point of
fasting. A continuous recognition of the self-destructiveness
involved balances this cheerless comedy. But the promise of
the work is not sustained throughout. The cheerless comedy
succeeds, but the turn to pathos and recognition of meaningless sacrifice is less powerful than it is meant to be. At the
crucial point Bennett abandons his direct presentation of the
miser, shifts the point of view to the servant Elsie, and fails
to make compelling Earlforward's sense of declining powers.

Earlforward is not, like Tellwright and Darius Clayhanger,
the fierce founder of the line. He is polite, reserved, consid-
erate--except on money matters. The atmosphere which he
creates is a caricature of the Five Towns predicament; he re-
strains joy, but there is no character in the novel to be restrained. Mrs. Arb shares his passion, though in lesser degree, and his undernourishment of her after their marriage
can hardly be tragic when she is so busily undernourishing
Elsie, the servant. But Elsie, though humorous and in her
way interesting, is not a character to whom restraint of joy
makes much difference; she is not going anywhere, as Edwin and Anna are; she will make out whatever happens, since
she is used to more sordid conditions than those at the Earlforwards'; she is really interested only in her shell-shocked
friend Joe. She is engaged in no serious struggle with the
Earlforwards, and the Earlforwards are apparently engaged
only in a test of how far home economy can be carried before
it becomes suicidal.

Nevertheless, *Riceyman Steps* is the best of Bennett's later
novels, partly because it has superior craftsmanship and partly because it is so much a satire rather than a disguised iden-
tification with an inadequate ideal. The structure has its own
cleverness and solidity. Part I, along with excellent description of the Riceyman Steps section, culminates Mr. Earlforward's courtship with the almost equally ascetic Mrs. Arb.
It also introduces Elsie and her background in the slums. Part
II, the most satirical section of the novel, shows Earlforward's
superb parsimony on his wedding day and ends, as usual in
Bennett, with a defeat--the defeat of Mrs. Earlforward's

plans for bringing order to the bookshop. Part III establishes
the ascetic tone of the Earlforwards' married life, and ends
in the defeat of Mrs. Earlforward's attempt to introduce steak
as a protection against their failing health. Part IV brings Mrs.
Earlforward to her collapse from a tumor and malnutrition,
and Part V takes Earlforward to his death, almost simulta-
neously with the death of Mrs. Earlforward. Malnutrition has
made it impossible for either of them to resist disease.

Much of the detail makes for effective realism. The creation
of a region equals anything in the descriptions of the Five
Towns; the sordidness of the area is set against Earlforward's
vision of "this wonderful Clerkenwell in which he lived." There
is Riceyman Square, the slum:

> Riceyman Square had been built around St. An-
> drew's in the hungry 'forties. It had been built all
> at once, according to plan; it had form. The three-
> storey houses (with areas and basements) were all
> alike, and were grouped together in sections by tri-
> angular pediments with ornamentations thereon in a
> degenerate Regency style. These pediments and the
> window-facings and the whole walls up to the be-
> ginning of the first floor were stuccoed and paint-
> ed. In many places the paint was peeling off and the
> stucco crumbling. The fronts of the doorsteps were
> green with vegetable growth. Some of the front-doors
> and window-frames could not have been painted for
> fifteen or twenty years. All the horizontal lines in
> the architecture had become curved. Long cracks
> showed in the brickwork where two dwellings met.
> The fanlights and some of the ironwork feebly re-
> called the traditions of the eighteenth century. The
> areas, except one or two, were obscene. The Square
> had once been genteel; it ought now to have been pic-
> turesque, but was not. It was merely decrepit, foul
> and slatternly.

But Earlforward, the antiquarian, daydreams of telling Mrs.
Arb of the true Clerkenwell:

He would explain to her eager ear that once Clerkenwell was a murmuring green land of medicinal
springs, well, streams with mills on their banks,
nunneries, aristocrats, and holy clerks who presented mystery-plays. Yes, he would tell her about the
drama of Adam and Eve being performed in the
costume of Adam and Eve to a simple and unshocked
people. (Why not? She was a widow and no longer
young.) And he would point out to her how the brown
backs of the houses which fronted on King's Cross
Road resembled the buttressed walls of a mighty
fortress, and how the grim, ochreish, unwindowed
backs of the houses of Riceyman Square (behind him)
looked like lofty, medieval keeps. And he would re-
late to her the story of the palace of Nell Gwynn,
contemporary of Louise de la Vallière. . . .

Like Big James with Edwin, he takes Mrs. Arb on a long walk:

In a few minutes they were at the corner of a vast
square--you could have put four Riceyman's into
it--of lofty reddish houses, sombre and shabby,
with a great railed garden and great trees in the
middle, and a wide roadway around. With all its
solidity, in that neighborhood it seemed to have the
unreal quality of a vision, a creation of some djinn,
formed in an instant and destined as quickly to dissolve; it seemed to have no business where it was.
    "Look at that!" said Mr. Earlforward, eagerly
pointing to the sign, "Wilmington Square." "Ever
heard of it before?"
    Mrs. Arb shook her astonished head.
    "No. And nobody has. But it's here. That's Lon-
don, that is! Practically every house has been divided up into tenements. Used to be very well-to-do
people here, you know!"
    Mrs. Arb gazed at him sadly.
    "It's tragic!" she said sympathetically, her bright
face troubled.
    "She understands!" he thought.

Coldbath Square surpasses even Riceyman Square in squalor,
but it is not romantic, nor is the interior which Mrs. Arb
sees when she visits "Elsie's home."

The quality of the novel appears most fully in the marriage
and the months following it. On the day before the wedding,
Earlforward files off Mrs. Arb's eighteen-carat ring (from
her previous marriage), trades it to a jeweler for a nine-
carat one, and insists that Mrs. Arb keep the profit on the
transaction. Mrs. Arb, to prove that she is worthy of such a
man, drives a harder bargain with Elsie than even Earlforward had dared suggest. But the climactic revelation of Henry's miserdom comes in the five chapters describing the wedding day visit to Madame Tussaud's. Henry feels that he has
already overspent before they enter Madame Tussaud's; the
ceremony and the wedding breakfast have been costly. He is
suspicious when Violet takes his pound note because she has
the right change for admission. He fears that the Cinemato-
graph Hall will cost extra, is vastly relieved when it does not,
but finds that the Chamber of Horrors, which Violet has come
to see, does cost eightpence, tax included. He cannot bring
himself to buy a catalogue of the Chamber and gets into difficulties by asking people who have one. Finally, he develops
trouble with his bad knee to avoid having to pay for the movie
which was to have climaxed the day's entertainment.

As even a summary suggests, some of this is broadly done:

> Withal, as he extracted a pound note from his
> case, he suffered agony--and she was watching him
> with her bright eyes. It was a new pound note. The
> paper was white and substantial; not a crease in
> it. The dim water-marks whispered genuineness.
> The green and brown of the design were more beau-
> tiful than any picture. The majestic representation
> of the Houses of Parliament on the back gave as-
> surance that the solidity of the whole realm was be-
> hind that note. The thing was as lovely and touching
> as a young virgin daughter. Could he abandon it for
> ever to the cold, harsh world?
> "Here! give it to me," said Violet sympathetical-

ly, and took it out of his hand. What was she going
to do with it?

"I've got change," she added, with a smile, her
face crinkling pleasantly.

He was relieved. His agony was soothed. At any
rate the note was saved for the present; it was stay-
ing in the shelter of the family. He felt very grate-
ful, but why should she have taken the note from
him?

. . . . . . . . . . . . . . . . . . . . . . . . . . . . . .

She sat him down in his desk-chair and as she dis-
pensed his tea she fluttered round him like a whole
flock of doves.

"Let me see," said he, with amiable detachment.
"Did you give me the account of that one pound you
had for spending yesterday?"

The best parts of the novel are the "adjustment" scenes between the mature newlyweds--the exchange of presents (Violet's hiring of cleaners to vacuum the house and books, Henry's presenting her a safe to keep her valuables in), the con-
troversy over mending the trousers, and the use of daylight
instead of even candlelight for mending. The climactic scenes
of their married love come in Violet's effort to force Henry to
eat steak to overcome his continued loss of weight. The tender
reconciliation that follows this quarrel becomes a mutual self-
revelation--of the hitherto guarded contents of their respective
safes. Henry is permitted to see and fondle the bonds in the
safe in the bathroom, and Violet sees for the first time the
banknotes and gold in Henry's office safe: "It might be hun-
dreds, it might be thousands. . . . How right he was always!
. . . She too ran her fingers through the gold . . . with the
faint radiance near the window from the gas lamp."

The first three sections of the novel are thus all, in their
way, satire on Earlforward. Even the excellent descriptions
of the slum area in Part I are satirical. But in Parts IV and
V the Earlforwards become the victims of disease, and, however much the disease may be their own fault, the reader
must shift his sympathy. Bennett is building toward the effect
that is made explicit after the two deaths:

Idlers sauntered about watching the gorging of the
pantechnicon and the erasing of T. T. Riceyman's
from the Steps. And what occupied their minds was
not the disappearance of every trace of the sojourn
on earth of Henry and Violet Earlforward but the
conquering process of that powerful and prosperous
personage, Charles Belrose, who was going to have
two shops and who would without doubt make them
both pay handsomely. Henry and Violet might never
have lived. . . .

So in Part V Elsie takes command, and the shift to her point
of view takes away much of the interest that might have con-
centrated on the ill Mr. Earlforward. For Elsie has her own
problems raised by the sudden return of Joe. She is able to
care for Mr. Earlforward only absent-mindedly. Part V therefore shows Elsie taking control of the house from Mr. Earlforward and establishing the sick Joe in her room. Her greater concern for Joe along with the new demands on her simple
mind begin to edge Mr. Earlforward out of his house and out
of the reader's attention before he has died--preparing for
his complete obliteration at the end of the book. In Part V the
reader has already begun to discount Henry and Violet Earlforward, and to take an interest in Elsie and Joe. Elsie has
two main characteristics, her humorous simple-mindedness
and her deep concern for Joe; both distract the reader from
the unfortunate condition of Mr. Earlforward. Earlier in the
novel the reader has seen "Henry" and "Violet" directly, from
their own points of view. But at the crucial point in the story
the reader sees only odd "Mr. Earlforward," who, to Elsie,
seems to be getting odder and yet more ineffectual than ever.
Even at the end Mr. Earlforward is still being presented
satirically. After Violet's death Mr. Earlforward makes the
supreme effort of getting dressed, and finds that Elsie has left
in his sacred safe a note saying that she has borrowed "6d":

Elsie's clumsy handwriting, which he knew so well
from having seen it now and then on little lists of
sales on the backs of envelopes! No! It was not the
loss of sixpence that affected him. He could have

borne that. What so profoundly, so formidably
shocked him was the fact that Elsie had surrepti-
tiously taken his keys, rifled the safe, and returned
the keys--and smiled on him and nursed him! There
was no security at all in the world of perils. The
foundations of faith had been destroyed. Elsie!
   But in the agony of the crisis he did not forget
his wife. He moaned aloud:
   "What would Violet have thought? What would my
poor Violet have thought of this?"
   His splendid fortitude, his superhuman courage to
recreate his existence over the ruins of it, and to
defy fate, were broken down. Life was bigger, more
cruel, more awful than he had imagined.

Mr. Earlforward's death is sandwiched between two chapters
on the hopes and schemes of Elsie and Joe.

Not only is there the remarkable structural narrowing, but
there is a corresponding retreat in characterization. Sophia
and Constance are great monoliths; but Hilda and Edwin represent expanded, more complex consciousnesses--a genuine
advance on *The Old Wives' Tale*. But the Earlforwards and
Elsie are a return to a simple conception of character; they
are, in fact, almost humor characters. Earlforward is parsimonious; Mrs. Earlforward is almost equally parsimonious
and so fearful about losing her money that she becomes Earlforward's victim; and Elsie is a comic servant whose consciousness is expanded somewhat for structural reasons. The
conception of Earlforward is frankly a devil-theory of obses-
sion--" the solitary demonic figure of Mr. Earlforward"; "the
monster recoiled and Henry wiped his brow"; "the monster
had come back upon him in ruthless might, to placate the monster he must at any cost bear Violet down." And Elsie's is
not an adult consciousness--she can be interesting only within
narrow limits.

But for all its failure to fulfill the promise of the Clayhanger
trilogy, *Riceyman Steps* belongs in the canon of Bennett's
half-dozen best novels. It is narrow and insufficiently ambiguous, but it has competent satire, an area of suggestion, and
a craftsmanlike realism.

# 10. The Pathetic Card

ALMOST all Bennett's critics have hoped to find a good later novel. Two candidates suggest an arrest, at least, in his decline. *Riceyman Steps* has the advantages of faintly symbolic realism, while *Lord Raingo,* for all its devices toward perspective, is basically an appreciation. It is the later Bennett's death of an aristocrat, an aristocrat who turns out to be the card, somewhat dignified by his peer's robes, but concerned with the same sort of "chicane" as Denry the Audacious. *Lord Raingo* and *Imperial Palace* both attempt to create a satisfactory myth of the man of power, and both suffer from a lack of esthetic distance. Bennett has no object other than the pathos of the strong-willed man cut down in his moment of triumph; there are no Orgreaves, no Dr. Stirlings, no English chaplains, but only men of Raingo's own world. There are no complex lines of kinships; Raingo is on guard against the world, even against his mistress, and in spite of some interest in his son Geoffrey, dies the big operator alert to trouble and betrayal. *Lord Raingo* is in actuality what some critics have tried to narrow *The Old Wives' Tale* down to--a story of time running out on a vigorous character.

Within these limitations, however, the novel has more vitality than any other of Bennett's later novels except *Riceyman's Steps.* Both the vigor of the card and the extremely detailed treatment of his death are memorable even though the kind of meaning which Bennett evolves in the earlier novels is now missing.

139

I

The character of Lord Raingo gives the first two-thirds of
the novel its force. Raingo, who has made millions in financial
manipulation, takes over the wartime propaganda ministry
and finds the supreme interest of his life in ordering its affairs
and promoting his own popularity. The spectacle of the most
highly developed practical mind brought to bear on the most
striking practical wartime problem gives Bennett an opportunity
to put to maximum use his wartime interest in administration.
Realist and worshipper of organization in his personal life,
Bennett admires Lord Raingo thoroughly.

A shift in technique emphasizes the extent of his sympathy.
The whole story, with the exception of seven pages, is presented from Raingo's point of view, and a portion of the writing
is a modified stream-of-consciousness. The ironical comments
of the author, conspicuous in *Clayhanger* and still present in
*Riceyman Steps,* all but disappear. Raingo appears through
action and his consciousness while in action. His moments
of introspection, until his illness, are rare; he is too busy,
and he is not the type. His comments on the action replace
the author's intrusions, and the irony that appears in all Bennett's novels here appears as Lord Raingo's irony. Bennett
can submit to the restricted point of view and the interior monologue, take his fling at writing a "modern" novel, because
he is willing to accept the leading character as his spokesman.
The values that Bennett wants to put into the novel are put in
through Lord Raingo.

The character of Raingo appears chiefly through interviews
and meetings in the first two-thirds of the book. We see him
first, in short chapters reminiscent of *The Old Wives' Tale,*
outbluffing the prime minister and gambling his chance at the
cabinet to win a place in the peerage. Then comes the impact
of his energetic mind on the new, but already hidebound bu-
reaucracy. He holds audiences in his office in big executive
manner. He makes an informal alliance with Mayden, the
hotel man representative of realism and efficiency as opposed
to the pomposity and timorousness of Sir Ernest Timmerson,
the official second-in-command; he goes through elaborate
chicane to keep Timmerson's dignity intact during this unan-

nounced shift of authority; he humors Eric Trumbull, the light
personality, in his desire to organize French propaganda clubs
for the dissemination of papers on "English Formal Gardens";
and he joyously twists the knife in Sir Rupert Afflock, the war
secretary, over a trifling interdepartmental jealousy. He en-
joys the whole procedure tremendously. Clyth, the prime
minister, speaks for all the leading characters when he coun-
sels Raingo:

> "As for the responsibility, the work is like any
> other work. It isn't a nuisance if you take pleasure
> in it. Can't be. And all this talk you hear about being
> only too willing to 'put down the burden of office' is
> insincere nonsense. It makes me sick. Look at me.
> Look at my responsibility. I'm game for it. I love it.
> World-war and so on--it's wine to me, it's women
> and song to me, lad."

All this has some vitality, but Bennett's effort to develop
perspective, to set the propaganda minister in his wartime
context, amounts only to having Raingo recognize that he is
fighting a paper war. The war is bringing delectable fame and
authority to a few; it is bringing its standard misery and death
to many. Bennett's device for keeping this irony before Raingo is to set elation over his successes against less happy
effects of war. His son Geoffrey returns from a German
prison camp with a nervous twitch and claustrophobia so serious that it prevents his sleeping indoors. Fresh from ap-
pointment as minister and promised elevation to the peerage,
Raingo comes upon the predicament of Mrs. Blacklow, the
clerk in his London office. Married to a prisoner of war, she
has become pregnant by another soldier whom she had known
for only ten days in a rooming house.

> This was the meaning of war. The meaning of war
> was within her. . . . One man fast in the arid rou-
> tine of a prison-camp; the other in a trench under
> fire. She had no home, only a lodging. The child
> ruthlessly, implacably growing, growing. And at
> the end of the war she would have to face the re-

leased prisoner; with the child. If the child did not
die. Another woman, desperate, might kill the
child or herself. But Mrs. Blacklow would be in-
capable of any such deed. She must wish that the
war would last forever. And he, Samuel Raingo,
was making the war into politics and intrigue. He
was not aghast at his conduct, for he perfectly understood that politics and intrigue are the inevitable accompaniment, as well as in part the cause,
of war. But he was deeply affected by the contrast
between the two aspects of war, as shown in himself
and in her. He became a speechless poet for a few
minutes.

Another glimpse of the same irony comes to Raingo as he
goes through the sit-stand-bow ceremony of becoming a lord.

"And this, too, is part of the war, " he thought,
with a sort of insane detachment. His uneasy mind
ranged over the immeasurable panorama of the war:
the ministerial departments contending with one another in secret, the altercations in the Commons,
the clangour of the factories, the bland disdain of
the imprisoned conscientious objectors, the private
agonies of the parents of young conscripts, Mrs.
Blacklow waxing with the baby not her husband's,
his wife toying with the idea of being presented at
court, Delphine dreaming in loneliness of love, sub-
marines under the sea and ships on the sea being
blown up, all the blood and mud and roar and shriek-
ing of the battlefields, and beyond the battlefields
the veiled lands where the enemy planned more de-
struction or yearned for peace at any price, and his
son Geoffrey, who had the guts to escape from these
lands and was now--somewhere.
"And here I am performing in a red dressing-gown
that cost me a hundred and eighty pounds!" thought
Sam. But not quite so crudely as it might seem, for
he well realized, beneath his nervous cynicism,
that the most preposterous contrasts are capable of

rational explanation, and that it takes every kind of phenomena to make a world.

So much, Bennett seems to say, for the rest of the world at war. There is the suffering of war--but look at the card's energy and organizing ability brought to bear on its departmentalized problems. War is a great game to the man running it, Bennett says all through the novel; but human nature makes that inevitable. Lord Raingo characteristically accepts the psychological facts even when they mean abandoning his grandly efficient scheme for uniting all secret service and propaganda under his ministry: "'Andy Clyth can't help it,' thought he, ruminating on the interview. 'He's got human nature to deal with, including his own. For all human nature cares a war is just like company promoting. And my human nature is not better than theirs.'"

## II

The second great value of the book, for Bennett, is Raingo's pneumonia. The narrative of the illness covers 132 of the 393 pages. In some ways this is one of Bennett's great death sections, but it differs significantly from the earlier ones. In the earlier novels, *Leonora, Clayhanger, The Old Wives' Tale,* death is a part of the fullness of life, an esthetic experience to the sensitive observer who looks at the dead or dying and sees the meaning of life as he has never seen it before. But in *Lord Raingo* there is no sensitive spectator, no Edwin, no Leonora, no Sophia. There is only death as the dying man himself sees it, a *mort intérieure,* a long wrestling, Job-like, with the accidental pattern of events which has brought him to his trial.

For Raingo is energetically ill. In bed with pneumonia as at his desk in the ministry, Raingo determines not to be self-deceived. He is alert to every indication of his condition in the voices of doctors and nurses, the attitude of Geoffrey, and the forced enthusiasm of the visitors. He jokes with the doctor, but in a moment is again the "speechless poet" (Auden this time) realizing that while disaster is preparing, "the donkey is scratching his innocent behind against a tree."

The poor, aging, plain nurse was healthy, was
going steadily about the daily business of existence.
He alone was the prisoner of disease, and suffered
the spiritual shame thereof. Everybody would soon
be condescending to him. . . . Andrew Clyth would
go ahead with his chicane and his will-to-win and
his ruthless egotism; the Cabinet would meet and
wrangle and decide; the Ministry of Records would
function, and all the other ministries and departments; the soldiers would fight--and he was laid
away futile and corrupted on his bed.

Raingo has flashes of insight into what seems at the time
the pattern of life. He sees clearly in the early stages of the
illness that he should have been careful:

Life was very illogical. No (he smiled philosoph-
ically in his pain), it was not illogical, it was merely long and had a long memory. Half a century ago--
some carelessness on someone's part, and he got
rheumatic fever! He recovered, but not his heart.
His heart had implacably waited for him, waited
for another bit of carelessness. He had been warned
and warned. Too stupid to take the warning seriously! In defiance of common sense he had strained
his heart, continued to strain it. He had left no
margins for accidents, and the accident of pneumonia had arrived. . . . That was all. Nothing illogical in it. . . . He had eaten the cake; the cake
was gone; it was not in his cupboard. The transaction of his life was as fair and as just as arith-
metic. Still, it was a damned shame.

He weighs his chances of recovering with his regular hon-
esty:

He thought he had read somewhere that more than
half the cases of pneumonia in men over fifty ended
fatally. (But even of that fact he was not quite sure. )

And many of the cases were not handicapped by a
weak heart. What chance had he, then? None. He
was sentenced. Yes, he had the chance conferred
by great wealth. He could and would receive the
finest treatment which the world of medicine could
offer. . . . But what was treatment against an un-
sound heart? And there wasn't a pin to choose among
doctors. The most celebrated of them were merely
creations of fashion. Mountebanks! Charlatans! Ingenious self-advertisers! In pneumonia a sound heart
was worth a hundred specialists.

But as the illness progresses, he wavers from both these
views. On the day before his death he gathers with his ther-
mometerlike sensitivity that the doctors do not expect him to
recover; he believes he will fool them and recover by will
alone. And on the morning of his death he sees his life in a different light; sees that, given another chance, he would act exactly as he had before.

What he obscurely desired was to review his life,
in a philosophical spirit. He had reviewed it days
ago--seemed months ago--and everything in his
life had held together logically then. He had blamed
himself then for taking risks which ought not to have
been taken. But the aspect of his life was not so
simple to him now. Why should he blame himself?
Circumstances had compelled him to take the risks
and to defy the commands of commonsense. The
point was--what was the point? He had once grasped
the point, but it was eluding him. Yes. The point
was: If he had to live his recent life over again,
would he have taken the same risks again? Yes, he
would. He would, he would. That was the point. He
was glad he had got the point clear at last. He was
not to blame, and he couldn't help that. He did not
understand God, and he did not understand life either,
and he wasn't going to bother. He was tired and
bored, and it was not his job to answer conundrums.

III

Lord Raingo carries the weight of the novel, but several
other characters are partly individualized--Andy Clyth; Tom
Hogarth, whom Winston Churchill identified as himself; Sid
Jenkin, the miner risen to the war cabinet and proud of it; and
Raingo's wife, Adela.

Adela and the members of the war cabinet are characterized
by different methods. The politicians appear predominantly
as in an O'Neill play, through dialogue and through Raingo's interior monologue. Raingo does comment to himself on Clyth a
good deal early in the novel, at Moze Hall, during the speech
on the manpower bill; but the prime minister becomes a more
nearly rounded character through the tug-of-war in the little
breakfast room, the barley soup drunk out of the same bowl,
the warning about the impending question in the Lords, and
the sickbed visit which helps bring on the final relapse. Jenkin, similarly, appears at the luncheon when Sam is being
looked over by the cabinet, at luncheon with Sam the first day
of Sam's ministry, at the party where Hogarth gets drunk, and
on his visit to the pneumonia victim. And so on.

By contrast Adela is characterized largely in the interior
monologue of Raingo, at Moze Hall, in the office in London, and
on the night of his elevation. She talks on all these occasions,
but her remarks assume significance as Raingo, thinking,
draws conclusions based on years of knowledge.

> A trifle, perhaps, unworthy of the notice of a
> statesman! But to Sam it was an awful symbol, typ-
> ifying the future as well as the past. She had after
> all no imaginative vision of a great event. Were not
> Lord and Lady Raingo, a Minister and his consort,
> dining together for the first time? She has never
> been a good hostess. Would she be equal to the po-
> sition of Lady Raingo? Despite her strange, un-
> deniable native authority she would not. . . . The
> title tied to her would be a mere ticket. Why had
> they no intimates and hardly any friends? Why was
> his wealth futile and ridiculous? Because she would
> not nourish friendship. On such a night friends ought

to have been dropping in or telephoning every few
minutes. Nobody had dropped in, and only two men
had telephoned--club friends who had no knowledge
whatever of Sam's home life.

The modernity of these techniques, compared to the Vic-
torian intrusions in such passages as "The Man-Child" in *Clayhanger* and the opening chapter of *A Man from the North,* is
obvious. But in adapting new methods Bennett retains many
of the old, especially in the handling of time.

The effect most frequently admired in *The Old Wives' Tale*
is that of time passing unnoticed and leaving its inexorable re-
sults. Bennett does not, in the later novels, reattempt this.
In *Lord Raingo* the effect is one of time slipping away with
ominous rapidity leaving much yet to be done. But the method
is reminiscent of *The Old Wives' Tale.* The short chapters,
four to six pages, each with its minor climax, reappear. But
the time lapse between them is much shorter than in *The Old
Wives' Tale*: the impression is of hurry and pressure. The
short chapters showing Raingo in conference, at Delphine's,
at the Savoy, at No. 10 Downing Street, at Moze Hall, and
back at the ministry pile up the effect of a man working constantly, living to the full extent of his energies, but lacking
the leisure to evaluate his activities or carry out equally pressing claims for action. It seems perfectly natural, therefore,
that his order forbidding military intelligence officers to enter his ministry, an order which Sam had laughed over as sil-
ly his first day in office, becomes a major issue and the cause
of his test before the House of Lords. And it seems equally
natural to find that he has realized subconsciously all along--
like Joseph at the bottom of the well--that he has been neglect-
ing the personal relations which would have avoided such a
crisis. The "Apotheosis" chapter, where Sam achieves his
highest success and catches pneumonia, has been prepared
for by a series of chapters that make his course seem as inevitable as he, in his last hours, believes it to have been.

But the effect in the last 132 pages is more complicated.
Bennett depends heavily on the device of making a section
dramatic by concentrating many pages on the action of a few
hours. So, in the description of Raingo's sickness, the time

lapses are clearly defined, and much shorter than before. The first day consumes six chapters, the night two, dawn one, and the second day three chapters--twelve chapters for the thirty-six hours. As in Dostoevski, the effect is to prolong time, here to give that indefinite stretching out that illness brings. But the prolonging does not result from lack of action. So much happens in the thirty-six hours that the reader who does not check assumes a much longer time is involved. In the first twelve hours Dr. Heddle, the new housekeeper, Nurse Kewley, Geoffrey, and Delphine's sister Gwen all require conversation. But Raingo's dramatic struggle is no longer to accomplish all that he has to do; the struggle is to talk and breathe--and keep up his remote control search for Delphine. The night is endless for him; he feels that if dawn will only come he can breathe. Day comes and with it Sir Arthur Tappit, the King's personal physician, and more activity. The many short chapters--each with its little problem and resolution, each punctuated by the nurses' presence, the sickroom routines, and the reiteration of Raingo's struggle to breathe-- build up the nightmarishness of the illness.

Once Bennett has established the full nature of pneumonia as a way of dying, he shifts quickly to the next phase, the passing of the first crisis. Chapter lxxiii begins: "Five nights later, and about a couple of hours later in the night, the patient noticed . . . that he was beginning to perspire." The day and evening following consume seven chapters. Raingo, certain that he is recovering, bears up through a series of sickroom visitors. Then, as he loses strength, the pace accelerates. Two chapters cover two days. The last thirty-six hours, again a period of concentration, require six chapters.

Two other characteristic methods add to the effect in *Lord Raingo*. Bennett draws upon the tricks of the trade to build up the characterization and verisimilitude. Mr. Povey is an early-day advertiser; Edwin Clayhanger brings his sense of orderliness to the printing business the moment Darius is incapacitated; Henry Earlforward resists his wife's cleanup of the shop because he knows the psychology of book collectors. And Lord Raingo knows from the first the tricks of publicity, banquets, big news, and bribery. He learns some of the tricks of

public office. These appear in such apparently slight touches
as in the Afflock interview:

> Timmerson, as the guardian of his own dignity,
> knew better than to run in immediately at Sam's
> summons. . . . Sir Ernest and Sir Rupert met with
> the loving exuberance of fast friends whom destiny
> had long been cruelly separating. They called each
> other Rupert and Ernest amid delightful shows of
> affection. Sir Ernest related his information about
> the order, treating it as a sort of family affray be-
> tween much-attached cousins, and not to be taken too
> seriously. Sam had instructed him in the method of
> approach.

And Sam understands the most important trick of the pol-
itician's trade the night he gets to drink broth out of the prime
minister's cup:

> Sam saw in a flash that Tom Hogarth was aston-
> ished and aghast at the degree of intimacy that exist-
> ed between him and the Prime Minister. He, Sam,
> had been seen drinking the Prime Minister's broth.
> Sam felt triumphant. He comprehended that po-
> litical power sprang as much from intimacy as any-
> thing. The minister who was on a footing to share
> the Prime Minister's broth was on a footing to in-
> fluence the Prime Minister with peculiar, perhaps
> unsurpassed, force. He had known the truth of the
> abstract principle, which was no more Oriental than
> Occidental. He now witnessed the concrete illustra-
> tion of it in the new glance of Hogarth's eyes, part-
> ly curious and partly respectful. And the situation
> had arisen solely out of the way in which Sam had
> first entered the room and greeted Andy, winning
> his sympathy at a stroke.

The other characteristic Bennett effect is incidental irony.
In *Lord Raingo* the commonest objects of this irony are politics and the medical profession. The medical part is mild in

tone, the political somewhat sharper. Thus Raingo is aston-
ished to see his own importance forgotten in the rush to make
everything convenient for the "arch-magician, " the King's
personal physician; the consultation of the two doctors produces, not a treatment for Raingo, but agitation over whether the palace will permit a *signed* bulletin. On the political
side are Raingo's comments on Clyth's speech, his failure to
recognize the name of his predecessor as minister, and his
discovery the first day of his ministry of the loneliness of
high office.

The concentration on a man of action largely removes the
slowness which exasperates many readers in Bennett. But
even here the kissing of the King's hand and the delivery of
the seals of office might have been omitted; the administrative
details of the middle section might have been telescoped. The
basic weakness of the novel, though, is its lack of perspective
and meaning--Geoffrey and Mrs. Blacklow are not quite
enough to carry the weight of irony they are intended to.

*Lord Raingo* is not only Bennett's last novel worth critical
consideration, but it also shows most clearly the nature of the
decline after the Clayhanger trilogy. In the period of his best
work Bennett wrote from the perspective of Fontainebleau, and
embraced both the vitality of the primitive and the aspiration
to the aristocratic which leads ultimately to some form of exile. But in *Lord Raingo*, as in the later *Imperial Palace*, Bennett identifies himself with the supercard.

The millionaire as a type character had always had two possibilities: to enlarge or to narrow the world. In his earlier
novels Bennett frequently separated his subtypes--Helen drives
toward a fuller life and Denry specializes in power. In Edwin
Clayhanger the drives conflict, and the success of his portrayal derives from the conflict. As a type the millionaire strad-
dles the polarization between primitivism and taste which I
have set up. He can be the man with the maximum freedom to
develop his noncommercial interests. But he can be the man
with the maximum opportunity and ability to control the immediate environment. He represents the possibility of carrying
on the bourgeois tradition intact, without the dispersing influence of culture. And this possibility had a great appeal to
Bennett, the more so as he became successful and influential

enough to have some contact with the world of power. Perhaps fortunately for the man, but unfortunately for his writing, he outgrew the tension between taste and a regressive primitivism, and found the significance of experience in characters who seem combined cards and miraculously reincarnated founders. As a promising novelist he values taste and culture as part of a rebellion; as an established novelist, he returned to--and modernized--the faiths of his father.

But he did not have a sense for the moral contradictions of power, and these later novels move in straight lines very unlike those of, say, Robert Penn Warren, whose sense for these contradictions is extreme. Bennett's problems and answers are straightforward. In the late novels the card has driven out the architect, and the questing millionaire has found his final answer: go back to work. The multiple levels become one.

# 11. Bennett and the Great Tradition

THE AIM of the preceding chapters has been to define the central meaning of Bennett's work and its place in the traditions of the century. If the analysis of the structural depth and the expansion of consciousness in his best work is sound, Bennett should rate a more important place in the canon of the twentieth-century novel than he does. I should go at least as far as F. R. Leavis and maintain that there is a great deal of life in the novels, though I naturally have gone farther than Leavis in attempting to say what kind of life it is. But Bennett is not a writer who has been, by an incredible error, left out of the great tradition, though he has never been fully understood. He does not have the complexity of perception and the distinction of style that mark the writer of the first rank. But if James's "registration of sophisticated human consciousness is one of the classical creative achievements, " Bennett's creative achievement is the registration of the semisophisticated human consciousness. (It is this achievement which, in spite of the tremendous structural complexity of *The Old Wives' Tale,* makes the Clayhanger trilogy his greatest work.) The line of mediation, the sophisticated primitivism, which includes Mann, the early James, Forster, and Joyce, and which comes down to Robert Penn Warren, is not an unwavering one; a definition which actually faced the differences and similarities within this line would be another book. But in trying to define the quality of Bennett's mediation between primitivism and taste I have certainly meant to say that Bennett is dealing

152

with important values and dealing with them in an important way.

There is a historical as well as an esthetic reason for the reaction against Bennett, which was more vigorous than his not-quite-great novels might have merited. Bennett's best work came just before the revolution in novel technique and interest of the twenties. Virginia Woolf's "Mr. Bennett and Mrs. Brown" did not destroy Bennett's reputation, but was a symptom of the new interest and was, as Mrs. Woolf all but says, a special plea for her kind of novel. The success of new modes of getting at consciousness in Joyce, Mrs. Woolf, Proust, Kafka, and the later work of Mann for a time gave evidence for a theory of progress about the novel. The great experimental novelists were seen writing not one kind of novel, but *the* novel. But these experiments of the twenties have become classic modern literature. Contemporary British novelists do not imitate Joyce, Lawrence, and Mrs. Woolf. In retrospect, the quality in all three which seems not quite of our time is an insistence, even laboriousness, about "forging anew the conscience of the race." The conscience--and consciousness--has unquestionably been forged and no one writes without being aware of it. But Henry Green, L. P. Hartley, Anthony Powell, Graham Greene, and Ivy Compton-Burnett assume a great deal which Joyce felt it necessary to spell out. The frequent problem now is of living with these assumptions. Taste, with its problems and possibilities of leisure, and primitivism, with its insistence upon native human nature, reappear as conflicting elements. So a quieter writer, like Bennett, with his sensitiveness to middle-class energy and "other-directedness," seems more at home in the fifties than he could have been in the twenties and thirties.

I have written about his decline as an attenuation of the major conflicts he was able to dramatize. But there is probably also this second reason. Bennett's talent was "objective." He saw personality as reflected in its surroundings, mannerisms, eccentricities, typical actions. In *Imperial Palace,* he came to demand perfect organization of these elements, undoubtedly out of a fear of the consequences of disorganization dealt with at such length in *Lord Raingo.* He wanted every object in its place, every action on schedule, every love affair according to the table of organization. An inflexible writer, he could not adapt to, and doubtless did not want to understand too well, the efflorescence of the inner life which his immediate successors developed. The interior monologue was suppressed in him and he could only suggest its existence. This technical inflexibility reflected truly his insensitivity to the new modes of understanding which the greatest novelists explored. But contemporary novelists assume an interior monologue and are interested in the apparently solid framework of social groups --so the emphasis on return to childhood, the nostalgia for class-conscious England, the playful concern with manners and social climbing. In this context of contemporary reality Bennett still seems old-fashioned, but relevant to the main conflict.

# Bibliography

### CHECK LIST OF BENNETT'S FICTION
(Starred titles reissued in Penguin editions, London, 1954)

*A Man from the North.* London: John Lane, 1898.
*\*The Grand Babylon Hotel: A Fantasia on Modern Themes.*
London: Chatto and Windus, 1902; Leipzig: Tauchnitz, 1902.
*\*Anna of the Five Towns.* London: Chatto and Windus, 1902;
Leipzig: Tauchnitz, 1912.
*The Gates of Wrath: A Melodrama.* London: Chatto and Windus,
1903; Leipzig: Tauchnitz, 1903.
*Leonora.* London: Chatto and Windus, 1903; Leipzig: Tauchnitz,
1912.
*A Great Man: A Frolic.* London: Chatto and Windus, 1904;
Leipzig: Tauchnitz, 1904.
*Teresa of Watling Street: A Fantasia on Modern Themes.*
London: Chatto and Windus, 1904.
*Tales of the Five Towns.* London: Chatto and Windus, 1905.
*The Loot of Cities: Being the Adventures of a Millionaire in
Search of Joy.* London: A. Rivers, 1905; Nelson, 1918.
*Sacred and Profane Love.* London: Chatto and Windus, 1905.
American title, *The Book of Carlotta.* New York: G. H.
Doran Co., 1911.
*Hugo: A Fantasia on Modern Themes.* London: Chatto and
Windus, 1906.
*Whom God Hath Joined.* London: D. Nutt, 1906; New York:
G. H. Doran Co., 1911; Leipzig: Tauchnitz, 1907.

*The Sinews of War: A Romance of London and the Sea* (with
Eden Phillpotts). London: Laurie, 1906; Leipzig: Tauchnitz,
1907. American title, *Doubloons*. New York: McClure,
Phillips, 1906.

*The Ghost: A Fantasia on Modern Themes*. London: Chatto
and Windus, 1907; Leipzig: Tauchnitz, 1907.

*The Grim Smile of the Five Towns*. London: Chapman and Hall,
1907; Leipzig: Tauchnitz, 1907.

*The City of Pleasure: A Fantasia on Modern Themes*. London:
Chatto and Windus, 1907.

*The Statue* (with Eden Phillpotts). London: Cassell and Co.,
1908; Leipzig: Tauchnitz, 1908.

*Buried Alive: A Tale of These Days*. London: Chapman and
Hall, 1908; Leipzig: Tauchnitz, 1908.

\**The Old Wives' Tale*. London: Chapman and Hall, 1908; New
York: Modern Library, 1931.

*The Glimpse: An Adventure of the Soul*. London: Chapman and
Hall, 1909.

*Helen with the High Hand: An Idyllic Diversion*. London: Chapman and Hall, 1910; New York: G. H. Doran Co., 1911.

\**Clayhanger*. London: Methuen and Co., 1910.

*The Card: A Story of Adventure*. London: Methuen and Co.,
1911; Leipzig: Tauchnitz, 1911. American title, *Denry the
Audacious*. New York: E. P. Dutton and Co., 1911.

*Hilda Lessways*. London: Methuen and Co., 1911; Leipzig:
Tauchnitz, 1911.

*The Matador of the Five Towns*. London: Methuen and Co.,
1912; New York: G. H. Doran Co., 1912.

*The Regent: A Five Towns Story of Adventure in London*. Lon-
don: Methuen and Co., 1913; Leipzig: Tauchnitz, 1913.
American title, *The Old Adam: A Story of Adventure*. New
York: G. H. Doran Co., 1913.

*The Price of Love*. London: Methuen and Co., 1914.

*These Twain*. New York: G. H. Doran Co., 1915; London:
Methuen and Co., 1916.

*The Lion's Share*. London: Cassell and Co., 1916; New York:
G. H. Doran Co., 1916.

*The Pretty Lady*. London: Cassell and Co., 1918.

*The Roll-Call*. London: Hutchinson and Co., 1918.

*Mr. Prohack.* London: Methuen and Co., 1922; New York: G. H. Doran Co., 1922.

*\*Riceyman Steps.* London: Cassell and Co., 1923; New York: G. H. Doran Co., 1923.

*Elsie and the Child: A Tale of Riceyman Steps and Other Stories.* London: Cassell and Co., 1924.

*Lord Raingo.* London: Cassell and Co., 1926.

*The Vanguard.* New York: G. H. Doran Co., 1927. English title, *The Strange Vanguard: A Fantasia.* London: Cassell and Co., 1928.

*Short Stories of To-day and Yesterday.* London: G. G. Harrap and Co., 1928.

*Accident.* Garden City: Doubleday, Doran and Co., 1928; London: Cassell and Co., 1929.

*Imperial Palace.* London: Cassell and Co., 1930; Garden City: Doubleday, Doran and Co., 1931.

*Dream of Destiny: An Unfinished Novel, and Venus Rising from the Sea.* London: Cassell and Co., 1932.

## SECONDARY STUDIES

The following list includes books on Bennett and a selection of chapters and articles which have at least some critical value.

### Books on Bennett

Allen, Walter. *Arnold Bennett.* (English Novelists series.) Denver, Col.: Alan Swallow, 1949.

Darton, Frederick J. H. *Arnold Bennett.* London: Nisbet and Co., 1915.

Johnson, J. G. *Arnold Bennett of the Five Towns.* London: Daniel, 1924.

Lafourcade, Georges. *Arnold Bennett: A Study.* London: Frederick Muller, 1939.

Massoulard, E. *Die romantischen Elemente in Arnold Bennett.* Bonn: Peter Hanstein, 1938.

Pound, Reginald. *Arnold Bennett: A Biography.* New York: Harcourt, Brace and Co., 1953.

Simons, J. B. *Arnold Bennett and His Novels*. Oxford: B.
    Blackwell, 1936.
Tresidder, Argus John. *Arnold Bennett: A Critical Study*.
    Ithaca, N. Y. , 1935.
West, Geoffrey. *The Problem of Arnold Bennett*. London: Join-
    er and Steele, 1932.

## Books Containing Criticism on Bennett

Drew, Elizabeth. *The Modern Novel*. London: Jonathan Cape,
    1926.
Forster, E. M. *Aspects of the Novel*. London: E. Arnold and
    Co. , 1928.
James, Henry. *Notes on Novelists, with Some Other Notes*.
    London: J. M. Dent and Sons, 1914.
Kettle, Arnold. *An Introduction to the English Novel*. New
    York: Hutchinson's University Library, 1951-53.
Muir, Edwin. *The Structure of the Novel*. London: Leonard
    and Virginia Woolf, 1928.
Orwell, George. *Dickens, Dali and Others: Studies in Popular
    Culture*. New York: Reynal and Hitchcock, 1946.
Priestley, J. B. *Figures in Modern English Literature*. Lon-
    don: John Lane, 1924.
Pritchett, V. S. *The Living Novel*. London: Chatto and Windus,
    1946.
Wain, John. *Preliminary Essays*. London: Macmillan and Co. ,
    1957.
West, Rebecca. *The Strange Necessity*. Garden City, N. Y. :
    Doubleday, Doran and Co. , 1928.
Woolf, Virginia. *The Second Common Reader*. New York: Har-
    court, Brace and Co. , 1932.

## Articles

Gide, André. "Arnold Bennett, " *La Nouvelle Revue Française*,
    XXXVI (1931), 727-29.
Howells, William Dean. "Speaking of Mr. Bennett, " *Harper's
    Monthly*, CXXII (1911), 633-36.
MacCarthy, Desmond. "The Popularity of Mr. Arnold Ben-
    nett, " *The Living Age*, CCXXI (1916), 251-54.

--------. "Notes on Arnold Bennett, " *The Living Age*, CCCXLIV (1933), 526-33.

Sherman, Stuart P. "The Realism of Arnold Bennett, " *The Nation*, CI (1914), 741-44, and CII (1916), 74.

Swinnerton, Frank. "Arnold Bennett, " *The Saturday Review of Literature*, IX (1932), 301-02.

Wells, H. G. "The Contemporary Novel, " *The Atlantic Monthly*, CIX (1912), 1-11.

Wilson, Angus. "Arnold Bennett's Novels, " *London Magazine*, I, No. 9 (1954), 59-68.